talking
about death
won't kill
you

talking about death won't kill you

Virginia Morris

Workman Publishing • New York

Library of Congress Cataloging-in-Publication Data

Morris, Virginia.
    Talking about death won't kill you / by Virginia Morris
        p.   cm.
    Includes index.
    ISBN 0-7611-1231-6 (hc)
    1. Death—Psychological aspects.   I. Title.

    BF789.D4 M65 2001
    155.9′37—dc21   00-069320

Cover and book design by Paul Gamarello

Workman books are available at special discounts when purchased in bulk for premiums and sales promotions as well as for fund-raising or educational use. Special editions or book excerpts can be created to specification. For details, contact the Special Sales Director at the address below.

Workman Publishing Company, Inc.
708 Broadway
New York, NY 10003-9555
www.workman.com

First printing July 2001
10 9 8 7 6 5 4

acknowledgments

Many thanks.

If you want to know who your real friends are, write a book. There you are, fretting about deadlines that you can't possibly meet, glumly acknowledging deadlines that have passed, taking about death . . . again, wondering why you ever took on the subject, and calling people in a panic because it has dawned on you that you will never actually finish this book. Good friends listen to all of this and love you anyway. I have truly incredible friends, and that is, without a doubt, why this book exists. To all of them, thank you, thank you, thank you.

I am indebted to a long list of experts who guided me along the way, especially Dr. Margaret Drickamer, Dr. Sherwin B. Nuland, Priscilla Ruffin and all the folks at East End Hospice, Dr. Kathleen Foley, Dr. David Weissman, and Dr. Joanne Lynn.

I want to thank, from the bottom of my heart, all of those who shared their stories, and their tears, with me. When you talk with someone about death, it removes any barriers, any distance that might otherwise exist. You become linked, on some level, for good. I couldn't be linked to a better bunch of people.

I am also deeply indebted to a few friends who not only supported me through this process, but read my manuscript, commented on it (pretty honestly, in some cases), and made it far better than it would have been otherwise. In particular, Tina Raymond, who read it not once, but twice, Marjorie Cave, Lou Ann Walker, Susan Merrell, Richard Ives, and Michael Shnayerson.

Enormous thanks and large bear hugs to my agent, Richard Pine, whose enthusiasm for this project fueled me and refueled me; to my remarkable editor and friend, Suzanne Rafer, who poured so much of herself into this that it's a wonder there's anything left of her; and to the ever calm and wise Peter Workman, who can count me as one of his many loyal fans. And to so many others at Workman Publishing, including my dear pal Jenny Mandel, who exudes energy and optimism, Jim Eber, Janet Hulstrand, and Paul Gamarello.

Last, but certainly most, I am grateful to my adorable husband, Bob Plumb, who doesn't particularly like talking about death but who has listened to me talk about little else for the past few years; to my irresistible children, who feed my soul; and to my incredible mother and siblings, who always believe in me more that I believe in myself.

Thank you.

For Marjorie Austin Morris,

my mom, my friend, my soulmate, my lifeline

contents

III avoiding common obstacles

IV brilliance in the shadow of death

a word of un-warning

reading about death won't kill you

Why read a book about death when the subject is so unnerving, when the mere mention of words like "lump," "malignant," and "chemo" can send a person's system into adrenal overdrive?

When I started this project a friend of mine called me, all upset. She felt that this endeavor was not only morbid, but dangerous. By studying death, she said, I might make it happen. A friend of hers had died of cancer while studying Portuguese death rituals. I, too, might be on a suicide mission. This subject was better left untouched.

Her concerns may seem a bit odd at first, but they are not unusual. Death is the boogeyman, hiding in the shadows of our bedrooms, arousing all sorts of anxieties and fears—some valid, some silly, some we don't readily admit even to ourselves. Most of us can't imagine the end of our existence as we know it. We dread the process of dying, the pain and disability. We panic at the thought of leaving loved ones, or having them leave us. "Afraid of death?" one friend responded incredulously. "Of course I'm afraid of death. I'm afraid of not being invited to a *party*. Death is the ultimate exclusion from the party, isn't it?" Whatever the particulars, all of us—the rich, the poor, the brilliant, the brave, the faithful, the atheistic, the young, and the old—all of us are touched in some way by fear and dread.

From a distance, when death is safely removed from our own lives, it intrigues us. But when it gets too close, too personal, we cast it quickly out of our minds and replace it with more palatable thoughts. As my brother-in-law said to me, "I am terrified of dying and there is *no way* I'm going to read your book." Why should he think about such a thing? Why should any of us think about it?

Why? Quite simply, because it is going to happen. Because we cannot avoid it. Because we will all die and virtually every one of us will witness the death of a parent or spouse or grandparent or sibling or friend. In all probability, we will not simply witness death, but we will be called upon to make critical decisions about medical treatment and daily care. We will have to decide how far to go and when to let go. And we will have to find some comfort and calm for our loved one, and for ourselves, amidst the storm. There is no escaping it, so we might as well have some idea of what we're in for and how we might best handle it.

But why bother to think about it now? Why not wait until some serious situation arises and then learn what to do? The problem is, once illness arrives, most people are too distraught, too overwhelmed by grief and disbelief, to think about how the end might come. A mother-to-be eagerly buys books about labor and delivery soon after the pregnancy test strip turns pink, but few people have any interest in learning about death right after the biopsy results come in. In fact, that is the last thing they want to learn about. A cloud of denial descends, distorting any ability to reason or to accept what is happening. And so, no matter what you might know in some logical corner of your brain, the rest of your brain, as well as your heart and your soul, are rooting for a cure, screaming loudly for an answer, a miracle, or a mistake. ("Oh sorry, those weren't your test results after all.") Coming face-to-face with the end of life is so surreal that unless you have thought about the issues, learned the possibilities, and talked to your loved ones in advance, unless all the fundamental information is there, you won't know what to do and you probably will not be open to hearing the options.

Hanging on the edge of a precipice, engulfed by terror, is not the time or place to learn about emergency rock-climbing procedures; you have to learn them before you start the expedition. Likewise, we have to start learning about death now, while we are still healthy. We have to start before illness is upon us, before we are in the swamp and our primal instincts take over, before we are blinded by denial and fighting valiantly for hope. We have to start today, whether we are twenty-eight or seventy-four, coming to terms with our mortality, understanding the medical choices that can arise, and developing an entirely new way of thinking about life and death.

Delving into a subject that is sad, scary, and largely taboo is difficult, there is no doubt about it. No one said it would be easy. But by bringing death out into the open, by witnessing it, talking about it, learning about it, and trying in whatever way we can to accept it as an inevitable part of our lives, we can be better prepared, we can make better decisions when the time comes, and we can change the way we die—for ourselves and for our loved ones.

*   *   *

What's interesting is that once you overcome your initial repulsion for this subject, learning about death really isn't scary, depressing, or dangerous. Although obsessing blindly about death is horrifying, learning about it is empowering. The thought of death will always fill us with dread. There is no escaping that. But the fear is less paralyzing, less blinding, when we have knowledge, when we can talk openly about it, and when we discover that we actually have the power to reshape it, to make it a more loving and rich experience.

Pulling death out from the shadows and examining it in the light does not make death happen. In fact, it does just the opposite. Thinking about death, learning about it and accepting it, makes life happen.

For many months now, after dropping my son at school, I have padded upstairs in my slippers to my office, sat in the morning sun with my lukewarm tea, and flipped through stories about people who have died and the people who have watched them die. I have driven around town with hospice workers, hung out in hospitals, called on people who are terminally ill, and talked to people who have recently lost a husband, wife, mother, or brother. I have entered people's lives at their most vulnerable moments, and seen, quite starkly, their fear, their helplessness, their love, and their despair.

Many times after these encounters, I have cried. I cry because I am sharing someone's grief and, in doing that, I am reliving losses I suffered in my own life and anticipating other losses I have yet to endure. But the emotion that wells up in my chest, and does so repeatedly despite my growing familiarity with this subject, cannot be described simply as sadness. It is more complex than that.

On the one hand, death exposes us. It strips us of all our protective layers and pretentious labels and takes us down to our cores, to the essence of who we are and what we feel. A prestigious job or big home or elite education has very little meaning when death is before us. None of these things can protect us from our final fate. They don't protect us from physical suffering or emotional distress. In the end, we are no different from the person standing next to us at the bus stop or the deli counter, we are no different from people on the other side of the world. Death reminds us that we are all human, we are all mortal, and in the end, we are all, each and every one of us, going to lose people whom we love, and we are going to die ourselves. This ultimate vulnerability, this shared destiny, links us together, hand in hand, and heart to heart.

The thought of death is also sad because it reminds us that despite all the daily complaining and bickering, we love people, we love life, and we do not want to say good-bye. How can we contemplate the loss of a spouse or a child? How can we begin to fathom our own demise, leaving those we love and then, what? Existing in some way that we cannot begin to comprehend, or perhaps not existing at all?

When we move beyond the fear, however, the picture takes on different hues. For what could make life more valuable than the simple fact that it is limited? What could make living more miraculous, more dizzyingly joyful, than the mere knowledge that we don't get to do it forever?

Hearing tales of death I am awakened abruptly from the numbness of daily life. My petty quests—for a bigger advance, or smoother skin, or a new living room rug, or whatever is on my mind that day—seem laughable. Suddenly my husband's embrace, my children's laughter, the smell of the damp morning air, even the familiar feel of the computer keys under my fingertips, are all so vivid, so terribly important and inexplicably wonderful. In the wake of my tears I find that the normalcy of life is not boring, but exquisite. I am no longer pinning my hopes on some better tomorrow or hurrying off to do something more "important," but living intensely for today, for this very moment. And what a glorious feeling that is.

Richard Sewall, an author and professor of English at Yale University, gave a talk soon after the death of his wife Mathilde, or Til, as her friends called her. I knew Til through my parents and their friends; the Sewalls lived not far from my childhood home and I had heard about them numerous times. After finding out that she was dying of pancreatic cancer, Til apparently became quite a wit, and enamored of life. Talking with a friend one day who was wishing nasty things upon a loathed politician, Til responded, "I am so full of love I can't wish harm on anyone." And then she added with a twinkle in her eye, "You know, if I should get well, I think I'd be rather nice."

In his talk, Richard said that his wife's final year "was the most educational year of my life, the high-water mark of my experience as a human being," for it was during that year that he learned not to be embarrassed about talking about love or about death. And it was during that year that he learned that the ending, sad as it is, is what gives meaning to all that comes before. Borrowing lines from Emily Dickinson, he explained, "There's something in the flight / That clarifies the sight. . . ."

If we allow death into our lives, if we open ourselves up to think about it and learn about it and be involved in it, we will open ourselves to thoughts and fears that are painful. But we might also find that our loved ones die a little better and that we grieve a little easier. And we might find, when we explore this subject in depth, that we love our friends and families a little more sweetly. We might appreciate what we have, and think less about what we want. We might have a little more patience for an irritable spouse or a belligerent child or an irritating coworker. Slowly it becomes clear that the urgent errands and concerns of the day—the late manuscript, the ugly hair, the cobwebs laced along the light fixture—aren't all that important. For life is short, and when we're taking in our last breath, the cobwebs are still going to be there and no one, but no one, will give two hoots. Confronting death, hearing the tales of others and imagining death in our own lives, makes us cry. It makes us grieve, it touches us in a place that is painfully human and wholly beyond our comprehension; but it also helps us to see the fragility of life, and in doing so, it helps us remember what truly matters.

Twenty years ago, I spent a summer in Newfoundland where I became friends with several local fishermen, simple men who wove their own nets and built boats from hand-hewn planks. These men had never spent a single day in school, nor had they ever paid taxes. The people of this tiny village, which was a long way from any hospital, doctor, or even a nurse, had seen death many times over and knew full well what it was about. One evening a few of us were sitting in a small living room, sharing stories and eating thick slabs of homemade bread smeared with black molasses, when I suddenly announced that I had to hurry off to finish some project or another. I can't even remember now what it was. One of the men shook his head slowly and said, in a wonderful deep brogue, "Aye, I don't have the time to hurry." The others nodded in agreement. I walked away, bewildered by this obvious contradiction. Now, all these years later, I know what he meant. Life is too short to rush through any part of it.

Before you read any further, I'd like to tell you what this book is, and what it is not. It is not a step-by-step guide on how to "die well," nor is it a handbook on how to create a "good death" for someone else. There are no quick solutions here; there are no to-do lists that will ensure you or your loved ones a better death. In fact, that is exactly the point of this book: There are no quick fixes. We can't

ge the way we die by signing a legal document or buying a bur-
plot. We can't draft a neat list of criteria outlining when we should
stop aggressive treatment and start hospice care. Changing the way
we die requires that we change the way we look at death. We have to
rethink our use of aggressive medicine at the end of life, certainly,
but we also have to do the much more difficult work of accepting the
fact that death does and will happen, and then opening ourselves to
both the agony and the intimacy which shape this passage.

This book attempts to help you do that. It is an exploration of the
experience of death—of how people die today, what options they
have, and what obstacles make dying more difficult. It also offers suggestions on how you might think about this subject and talk about it
with your loved ones. My goal is not to tell you what to do or what
decisions to make, but rather to give you a glimpse of the process and
to get you thinking about all that lies ahead, so that you are not taken
completely unaware when death crosses your path—whether the person who is dying is you or someone you love.

Also when I tell the stories of dying people in these pages, it is not
to show what was done wrong or right, but simply to illustrate some of
the things that happen. For there is no "right" way to die any more
than there is a "right" way to live. There is no prescription for the
masses. We will each have to handle disease and death in our own
way, finding what works for us and our families in that moment.

Death will never be easy. It will always cause suffering. We will be
overcome by sadness and disbelief. We will be uncertain about what
to do. We will wonder, if we are the survivors, if there wasn't something more, something different, that we could or should have done.
We can't avoid those questions. But by learning the choices and
opportunities that frequently arise, and bracing ourselves for the
losses we will face, we can soften the dying process. We can make

death a little gentler, perhaps more meaningful, and for some, even extraordinary.

So read on. This book is not harmful to your health; it will not cause birth defects, or cancer in laboratory rats. It cannot cause death or depression or disease. But it might change the way you die, the way your loved ones die, and the way you experience and then grieve those deaths. And who knows? It just might change the way you live. It did for me.

jack

one birth, one death

When I became pregnant several years ago, there was no shortage of advice. Sisters, friends, and people I hardly knew told me what to eat, what to wear, how to exercise, and which doctors or midwives to see. They told me which medications and treatments to accept during labor and which to avoid, when to crouch, when to walk, and how to breathe. They told my husband what he was about to witness, how to time the contractions, and how to help me through each agonizing one. They shared their own experiences and lent me books and videos so that I could do it "right"—that is, without surgery and, if at all possible, without drugs. Giving birth, they said, is not a medical procedure to be left to doctors, but a natural event, a glorious celebration of life, an initiation into womanhood.

For the most part, they were right. The birth of a baby is glorious. It is a celebration. Of course, it is also incredibly painful, frightening, and loaded with physical indignities. But despite all that, the beginning of life is a miracle, and I found that all the advice and preparations only helped to make it more of one.

I learned something else, quite unexpectedly, during those nine months. Three months before my son entered this world, my father left it, and I discovered that despite the pain, fear, and indignities that go with it, death is also a rite that should not be left to doctors. It, too, can be a profound celebration of love and life. Even more of one than birth. After all, my father had many years of living to celebrate. And his death, much more than my son's birth, served as a potent reminder of just how precious life is.

My father had advanced prostate cancer which, after more than four years of being assaulted with drugs and radiation, had launched a final, all-out attack, spreading throughout his body and lodging itself deep in his bones. My father was a gynecologist who specialized in surgical oncology (the treatment of cancer), so he knew exactly what was happening to him. Ever so slowly, the rest of us came to understand what he already knew.

Several months before my father died I sat in a church pew, flanked by two of my sisters. My grandmother, at age 98, had died in a nursing home and we were sitting through an impersonal and poorly attended funeral service. My father was in front of us, sitting next to my mother, listening intently. My sisters and I were barely listening at all. Our attention was focused on Dad. He sat erect, still, and calm. The hair on the back of his head was sparse, light gray and silky soft, his neck slender but strong. As I gazed at that neck I could almost smell the skin, warm and comforting, a place where I had buried my face many, many times. But what drew my eyes to this spot, what the three of us remember to this day so vividly, so painfully, was there, on the back of his head, at his hairline: a stark blue T penciled onto his skin, a target for beams of ionizing radiation. A tattoo marking his disease, marking his future, and marking ours as well. It was slowly dawning on us as we sat there that the next funeral we attended would most likely be his.

Three months later, on a Friday afternoon in early March, my father had a small, imperceptible stroke that, we learned later, had damaged his peripheral vision. His cancer was raging and although he had rejected chemotherapy before, he was now racing to the hospital to begin a drug regime, in a last desperate attempt to survive. With his compromised peripheral vision, he bumped into a car and banged his head on the windshield. Bruised, he drove on, got his chemo and then, on the way home, hit a second car and smacked his head into the windshield yet again. This time, however, the damage was serious, and he was taken by ambulance back to the hospital, where he stayed overnight.

Dad came home the next morning. The cancer was beyond control and now, with a grotesque, multicolored bulge extending across the top of his head as a result of the car accident, he was fading fast. He could barely get up and down the stairs, his appetite was gone, and most noticeable, his spirit—an unbending will that had brought him both respect and ire over the years—was broken. He looked quietly at the floor as I talked to lawyers and insurers about the accident, explaining that he would not be making any court appearances.

Several days later, he sat in his favorite chair in the living room and I sat on the floor by his feet. I was urging him to eat some scrambled eggs that were growing cold. "No, I can't," he said. "I'm not hungry." Then he added, quietly but matter-of-factly, "This is what happens in the terminal stage."

A protective wall that had stood between us shattered. He had never acknowledged his dying so bluntly with me before. His comment left us in silence for a long moment, and then, realizing that the opening was still there, I said quietly, "Are you afraid?"

He paused. "No. No, not afraid. I just want to be sure that your mother will be okay."

"We'll take very good care of her," I assured him. But I didn't venture any further. This territory was too foreign and too painful.

For the rest of that day Dad was withdrawn, perhaps resigned, driven only to do some final-hour sorting of papers at his desk. Late in the evening—maybe that evening, maybe the next; it's so hard to remember—Robert Gordon, a family doctor who was also a longtime family friend, stopped by. After a quick examination, he stood at the foot of the stairs, his hand resting on the end of the railing, and told my mother and me that it was time for us to call hospice.

Hospice. The word shot through us like a dagger. Dr. Gordon's own pain was visible as he took his coat and walked out the door without another word. My mother and I stood in the dimming light of the early evening as the door clicked shut, and looked at each other for a moment, stunned, before we fell into each other's arms and began sobbing uncontrollably.

In the last weeks of his life, my father grew visibly weaker every day—he was unable to walk to the toilet unaided, then unable to walk to the toilet at all, finally unable to sit up on his own. His skin, which clung loosely to his increasingly angular frame dulled to a whitish-gray. He ate almost nothing, just a few small refreshing tastes of lime sherbet and sips of cool tonic water, which we sometimes bolstered with a bit of gin. With time, his breathing became labored. His fingertips, toes, and the end of his nose grew cold, and then, as the days slowly passed, the chill spread from his extremities toward his chest.

My father, it seemed, was dying from the outside in. And I was watching it happen.

Some of my most vivid childhood memories are of my father leaving. It was Saturday afternoon, Sunday morning, summer vacation, Thanksgiving, Christmas, and my father had to go see a patient, do some paperwork, meet with residents, attend a meeting. He would drive down the driveway, one arm extended, waving wildly, and we would return the gesture from the garage, the kitchen window, the front lawn. He waved good-bye as he walked down airport terminals. He waved good-bye as his boat pulled away from the dock at our summer cottage. He waved good-bye at the train station. This image was so clear to me during those weeks, so painfully familiar. Him leaving, waving good-bye, disappearing from my life, shrinking to a dot until, squint as hard as I might, I couldn't see him anymore. Now it was happening again: he was leaving, slowing shrinking away, this time for the last time.

He was a demanding father, but that was his way of showing love, his way of adoring us—always pushing us to try harder, to do more, to be better, and to never, ever give up. He didn't accept mediocrity. Not from himself, not from us, not from anyone. Dad loved us with a passion and he was proud of us when we succeeded. But unlike our mother's love, which was unwavering, Dad's love felt conditional at times, ebbing and flowing with the tides of our achievements and failures, and sometimes deserting us when we needed it most.

He was a busy man. Busy with critically ill patients, with cancer research, with international conferences; busy with things that were more consequential than a school play or a hockey game or a Girl Scout dinner, things that were more urgent than a sprained ankle or a teenager's insecurities. He was fun and silly at home, playing the piano, dancing a jig, making crazy cocktails for us, baiting us to push him into the pool, but more often than not, he felt his time with us Mattered. He talked to us about Life Decisions. He never understood that when it comes to kids, listening is better than talking, and long phone calls about nothing can be the most important conversations of all.

My four siblings and I returned to our childhood home to care for Dad, to finally have time with him doing nothing, and to say good-bye. We took turns wiping his body with damp washcloths, dressing him in fresh pajamas, adjusting his pillows, moisturizing his dry lips, conferring with nurses, and adjusting his morphine. When he could barely speak, we spoke to him. We told him about the friends and col-leagues who called and wrote and sent flowers and food, we relived our family trips to Stony Lake and to various beaches along the Con-necticut and California shorelines, we sang silly songs that he had taught us as children—always hopeful, but never certain, that our voices gave him comfort.

Most of the time he lay silently, his eyes closed, semiconscious. Occasionally he muttered his way through an entire surgical proce-dure, giving one final list of instructions to imaginary residents and other young doctors. But a number of times his eyes opened, wide and alert, and he joined us briefly in a song, or he said something funny, or he stared intently at one of us and said, with a deep sigh, "Oh, darling," as if he had never known such love before. And hon-estly, I believe he never had.

Faced with death, my father let go of his paternal control and allowed us, for the first time, to care for him. He let go of his anger, intolerance, and frustration. Black Jack, the Old Goat, the Grump. No, now my father was gentle, warm, and full of love. He was the man who had always been hidden there, buried beneath the gruffness of life.

My siblings and I also found tenderness in the realm of death. We, too, gave up any expectations or resentments we might have had. During those weeks, we loved him intensely and forgave him completely. Life was too short, too dear, to do anything else. And the truth is that despite any of his shortcomings we did love him. Fiercely.

A day or two before my father died, during a brief lucid moment, he asked for my mother, a woman with whom he had spent more than half of his life. She came upstairs, sat on the edge of the bed, held his hand, and looked expectantly into his eyes. But no words were spoken. None were needed. They stared at each other, then into each other, and in that moment the world around them ceased to exist, and they became one person, one soul, swimming, swirling, loving, and dying together. After 42 years of living together, side by side, they knew each other better than they knew themselves, and they were able to look directly into each other's hearts, able to make love, to define love, to say this last good-bye, with their eyes.

After that, he began to let go of his grasp on this world. His breathing became irregular, teasing, uncertain. And so did ours. In. Out. In. Out. In. Out. Silence. Silence. Silence. Huge in. Out. We held him. We caressed him. We continued to reminisce and laugh and love on some other plane, higher and deeper and sadder than we had ever been before. We watched and we listened; we watched and we waited. For what, I'm not sure we knew. And then, at five o'clock on an unusually warm April afternoon, a loud gurgling, rattling noise escaped from my father's chest and his breathing stopped. Completely.

My sister screamed out. No, Daddy. No. No. Don't go! Please don't go! My brother ran to his side. I stared, frozen for a moment. And then I crawled across his king-size bed, put my lips near his ear, and followed the only advice I had been given in all those months. I let my father go. I told him not to be afraid. I told him that he was safe and didn't have to fight anymore. I said that he should go in peace. I said that he was surrounded by love. I said that we would miss him terribly, but that we would be all right. It's okay. It's okay. The words poured out of me faster than I could follow them. I wanted so desperately to send him on his way as he had sent me on my way many times before—with comfort, confidence, and love.

Then my rush of words stopped. My sister's wailing hushed, my mother lifted her head from her hands, and my brother sat back in his chair. The room was still. Dad's head was tipped back slightly, his eyes stared blankly toward the ceiling, and his jaw hung open. The morphine pump lay beside him, still on. My father was dead, his body lifeless. I stroked his cheek, brushed a few wisps of white hair back from his forehead, and kissed his neck. I curled his big, soft hand around mine. And then I put my head on his naked chest and sobbed. My father. He had loved me, infuriated me, taught me, and fought me. And now he was gone. Forever.

Just three months later my son came into this world. Pulled from my belly, his pale, wet body was placed on my naked chest. He cried and flailed his tiny arms and gasped for air, until his eyes met mine for the first time, and then he relaxed into a long and magical gaze. My little boy. My baby. Jack. Named after the grandfather he would never meet. For the second time in those brief months, I experienced a love, an intense and pure sort of love, that I had never known before.

A new life arrived, an old one departed. Both passages were draining, physically and emotionally draining. Both were loaded with indignities and pain. But I would not have missed either experience, not for anything in the world.

*   *   *

For the most part, my family was lucky—lucky that we knew that Dad would not want to be in the hospital or to have his dying prolonged; lucky, oddly enough, that he had become so sick that no real thought was given to continuing chemotherapy or radiation; lucky that no one in the family held false hopes or insisted on further treatments; lucky that we could leave our own lives behind and be there to care for him. We were fortunate to run into a dear family friend, a medical colleague of my father's, who reassured us that we were doing the right thing and told us to give Dad all the morphine necessary to keep him comfortable. We were blessed to have another friend arrive at our front door with much-needed groceries and a little advice on how to care for him, how to love him, at this time. And so, with luck and a few bits of good advice, we bumped along, learning as we went, and stumbled, more or less, onto a good death.

We were lucky. But we were not prepared. We didn't know what to expect—how his disease might progress or what decisions we might face—or how we might handle any of it. When I was pregnant, I studied, practiced, and tried to imagine labor and delivery. I talked about it with friends, heard about their experiences, and got untold amounts of advice. But when my father had a life-threatening illness, I did nothing of the sort. I didn't look things up or ask questions. My family didn't even acknowledge—not in any meaningful way—that my father was going to die until he was almost gone. Most of the time we tiptoed gingerly around the subject or jumped clear of it.

For years I knew that Dad was very sick and that, sooner rather than later, he was going to die from this disease. But I pushed that information back into some recess of my mind and ignored it. It was easy to ignore because no one talked about it—not family, not friends, not doctors, not even my father. Oh, we talked about CAT scan results and prostate-specific antigen levels and, among ourselves, we acknowledged that this was serious, that probably he wouldn't be around next Christmas. But we never, ever, talked about the process of his dying and how we were going to manage it. We never talked about how we would care for him, how we could keep him at home, how we might patch up any tears in our relationships with him, or how we might make his last days more comfortable. We never asked him about his fears, his needs, or his wishes so we never knew how he felt, except for what he revealed in one or two brief comments he made during those final days. We never talked about what we were about to lose, how that loss would occur, how we would say good-bye, or how very much we would miss him.

Why was I so afraid to say the "D" word, and especially afraid to say it to my father, of all people? As if he didn't know what was happening, as if any mention of death would alert him to a closely guarded secret. What was I thinking? He had cared for people who were dying of cancer throughout most of his life. Of course he knew what was happening. Perhaps I was silent because I had never seen anyone die, and had never spoken in any depth about death—about the process of dying—before. Perhaps I was silent because this is the way dying is dealt with in our culture, as if it were something dirty, something not to be mentioned by polite people, something that, if said aloud, might upset someone. And perhaps my friends were silent because they, too, didn't know how to broach such a topic or offer support. Maybe this is just how we all enter the realm of death.

I have since learned that this is a common response, and for people who are not so lucky as I was, this blind approach can have dire, lasting consequences. I didn't intend to learn any of this. In fact, for a brief time, I tried to do just the opposite. I tried to run away from this subject. But somehow it kept coming back to me.

After my father's death and my son's birth, I was haunted by thoughts of death. I thought about my own death, for the signs of my own aging were now rampant: sprouting skin tags, deepening lines, a sprinkling of white hair, and an odd twitch in my little finger, a tic that I first saw in my grandmother, then in my mother, and now in me. In the solitude of the night, when the house was quiet and my anxieties had free reign, I was certain that a headache meant trouble, or that any intestinal pain was a sign. I was sure that I was about to be handed bad news. Lump. Malignant. One year, maybe two, tops. I couldn't shake the obsession, couldn't escape the foreboding.

I also thought about the eventual death of my mother. My mother has been with me through every up and down in my life. When I was little and couldn't sleep, she would sit on the edge of my bed and gently stroke my hair until I drifted off. When I was a hormonal teenager, confused and crabby and not fit to be around, she hugged me and believed in me. I told her all my secrets and, when I was old enough to understand them, she told me many of hers. My mom. My guardian angel. My soulmate. She was still active and fully independent, but in the wake of Dad's death, engulfed by grief and solitude, she grew old quickly. Her hair thinned, and her already slim body began to reveal her bones. It came as a shock: My mom was mortal. She was going to die one day. And I was going to be left on this earth feeling very, very alone.

What haunted me more than anything else during those months, however, was the question of how my son would survive if I were to die. With his birth, I was given a reason to live that I had never had before. I was grown up and, despite whatever grief I might face, I knew I could handle the death of a parent. But how would this tiny little boy cope if I were to die? Who would raise him? Who would comfort him? My husband is a good father, but could he be a mother too? Would he marry someone who would love my child? And what horrific memories would my son have of me from those final months, if disease and drugs turned me into a puny, puking invalid? Who would teach him all the things I wanted him to know? Who would be there for him when he needed a mother's love? How would his psyche and future relationships be mangled by having lost his mother so early in life?

I was okay during the day, but sometimes in the middle of the night dread would swell in my gut. It was ridiculous. It had to stop. I vigorously pushed these morbid thoughts out of my head, and finally, I escaped them, more or less.

I escaped them until I had to write the final chapters of a book on caring for elderly parents, one chapter on death, and one on grief. Now I had no choice. No out. I was going to have to read about death, talk to people about death, and think about death. I was going to have to face this thing, like it or not. As it turns out, I'm glad I did.

I
dying today

unhappy endings

death is often painful and lonely

As I did my research, I heard about people like my father, who had softened and opened up and generally become "more"—more real, more loving, more serene—as they neared death. I heard about broken relationships that were repaired and about love that was intensified. I heard about people who were prepared to die and were very much at peace. And I heard about family members and other loved ones who found that caring for a dying person, while extraordinarily difficult, was a rich and gratifying experience that changed their lives. They said they were less afraid of death, they appreciated life more, and they were prepared to help other family members and friends who might face a terminal illness. I still have a beautiful picture in my mind, left there by a woman who had spent many days at her father's bedside before he died: "I spent a lot of time up in his bedroom at the end," she said. "The late November sun would come in the window, and while he lay in bed I sat at a card table writing poetry, with the fire blazing. We had a profound relationship. . . . He became very open and tender. We could talk about anything."

The vast majority of the stories I heard, however, were not so lovely. People told me about their loved ones, usually a parent, dying in a hospital or nursing home after years of illness and disability. Most of them had little to say about the death itself except that the patient had suffered terribly and, thank God, he or she was finally out of pain, or free from dementia, or at rest. Some had lost a family member suddenly and were left stunned, grappling with the abrupt dissymmetry in their lives. Many people talked about opportunities they had missed and actions they regretted. They were bewildered by their own inability to see that death was imminent, hurt by a medical system that had failed to help them through this process, and mired in grief because they didn't get to say good-bye to their loved ones, not in the way they wanted to.

"Why didn't I know? *Why?*" a woman said to me one day, choking on her own tears. Her mother had been hospitalized for end-stage emphysema, and yet death was never discussed—not by the doctors, not by the family. In fact, she said, her mother's primary physician offered little but hope, talking with them about new treatments and how well her mother was doing. Based on all this optimism, the daughter packed up her family and moved from France to the United States shortly before Christmas in order to be home for what she thought would be her mother's remaining years. Her mother died only days after the move, in the hospital and in pain. "I never got to tell her what I felt," the daughter sobbed. "I never told her how much I loved her. I never realized what was happening."

Never realized, never knew, never expected. . . . These are the words I heard over and over again. People thought that because their loved ones had made it clear that they didn't want death dragged out, didn't want to be "hooked to machines" when the end was near, that they would die in some other way. They didn't realize that it doesn't happen like that; it simply isn't that easy.

When Katherine Denny's husband, Jerry (both names have been changed to ensure privacy), was diagnosed with emphysema and a damaged heart, the couple sought out the best medical care possible. They selected the most prominent hospital in the area and lined up a team of top-notch doctors. Katherine cared for her husband with devotion. She went to his medical appointments every six weeks for three years. She monitored his medications. She conferred with his doctors. And she promised her husband that when the time came, she would never, ever, drag out his death.

But she didn't prepare herself to carry out that promise. She and her husband didn't discuss exactly what that meant, what he wanted and what he didn't want, or how they might achieve his goals. They never spoke with people from a hospice program or talked to the doctor about how they might handle an emergency—and emergencies are to be expected when someone has severe lung or heart disease. Katherine had made a promise, like so many of us do, without any understanding of what it would take to keep it.

So when Jerry lay on a stretcher in the emergency room, pale and frightened, frantically whispering, "I can't breathe," and the emergency room doctor turned to Katherine and asked, "Do you want us to put him on a machine?" she stood, frozen in place. She had no idea what he was talking about. "What kind of machine?" she recalls thinking.

"Jerry and I had promised each other never to allow extraordinary medical procedures. No life support," she said later, recalling that fateful moment. "He was definitely a sick man. I knew that he would die of these problems. But I didn't know that, given his situation, life support was likely to be in our future. I was never told that for a person with breathing problems, in an emergency situation, a respirator would be indicated. They never told me what it was like. We had this general idea that we didn't want to be on machines, but as far as specifics go, we hadn't discussed it."

Katherine didn't know that had they anticipated and prepared themselves for this moment they might have agreed in advance that a respirator could be used only for a trial period and then removed if Jerry didn't show improvement. Or she might have skipped the respirator and opted instead for treatments aimed solely at comfort, such as a course of bronchodilators, painkillers, sedatives, oxygen, and perhaps some relaxation therapy to ease his distress. She didn't know that she and Jerry could have had those final moments, which might have been minutes or hours or days, to hold each other, instead of being separated by machines. She didn't know.

"I heard the click of the minute hand from the wall clock," Katherine recalls. "In fifteen minutes, unless I said 'yes,' Jerry would be dead."

Jerry gasped for air. Katherine said, "Yes."

"And I never heard his voice again," she says. Once he was hooked to the respirator and a number of the other devices that typically accompany a respirator—heart monitors, intravenous lines, feeding tubes, oxygen monitors—Jerry could not speak. And he could not rest. Like many patients, he tugged anxiously at the tubes surrounding him, finally dislodging one of them. To stop him, the doctors lashed Jerry's arms to the sides of his bed. Imprisoned, he panicked. He lunged forward repeatedly, trying to free himself. He looked at his wife pleadingly. She begged the doctor to sedate him. He was given medication, but it provided little relief. The doctor explained that further medication might compromise his breathing, so they couldn't give him very much.

Katherine felt utterly helpless. She stayed by Jerry's side 16 hours a day, agitated and unhappy, not knowing how to help or what to do. The only thing she felt she could do for her husband, to care for him in his hour of need, was to dip a swab into a glass of water and wipe it in his mouth to relieve the dryness.

After 20 days of this nightmare, Jerry died. One year later, Katherine still cries when she recalls those final weeks. "I watched my husband being tortured in front of me," she says, pausing to control her tears. "He tried to communicate with his eyes. His eyes were pleading all the time. I could hardly touch him because there were tubes everywhere. His arms were tied. One day a doctor came in and saw me stroking his calves and he said, 'Oh, he's getting a massage.' But I was touching him there because that was the only place where I could touch him. I couldn't even touch his face." Katherine becomes silent for a moment. "Those are my memories," she says. "That is what I am left with."

I wish I could say that this was the odd story, the unusual case, an extreme. But distressing tales like Katherine's, and the resounding grief that accompanies them, are not just common; they define the majority of deaths in America today.

Although 90 percent of people say they want to die at home (according to two Gallup polls), nearly 80 percent of people die in hospitals, nursing homes, and other institutions. These people are not in a comfortable, soothing environment surrounded by loved ones during their final days of life; most of them are hooked to tubes and encircled by machines, glaring lights, and strangers in blue scrubs who, for the most part, try to avoid them. According to one major study, shortly before death, about 40 percent of hospitalized patients spend 10 days or more in an intensive care unit, where the lights are brighter, the noises louder, and the intrusions more frequent. They are distanced from family and often separated from their primary doctor, who has been replaced by a specialist or by a doctor assigned by a nursing home, a person with whom they have no relationship. They have little control over their care, their daily life, their sleep habits, their meals, or even whether the window is opened or the curtain drawn.

Research on how people die is scarce, but the studies that have been done, as well as firsthand accounts, make it clear that the majority of people today die in pain, struggling with a litany of symptoms. The study mentioned above, known as the Study to Understand Prognoses and Preferences for Outcomes and Risks of Treatment, or SUPPORT, included more than 9,000 patients with life-threatening diseases at five U.S. hospitals, making it the largest study of death ever undertaken. The researchers found that 50 percent of patients were conscious prior to death, and of those, half were reported to be in moderate to severe pain most of the time. In addition to their pain, patients typically were overcome by intense fatigue. Many suffered from shortness of breath, a terrifying symptom. Most struggled with other agonies as well, including confusion, nausea, skin sores, constipation, infections, dry mouth, and itchy skin. And many run through the bulk of their life savings paying for such medical care during these final months or weeks of life. When Dr. Joanne Lynn, the lead investigator of the study, looked within her own hospital in Washington, D.C., she discovered that more than a quarter of patients also died with their arms lashed down at their sides to keep them from pulling at the tubes that so irritated them.

Although most patients say they want care that is focused on comfort, more than half of those people in the study received aggressive life-sustaining treatment, such as a resuscitation attempt or the insertion of a feeding or breathing tube, within three days of dying. Only 14 percent of patients had signed some sort of advance directive—a living will or health care proxy outlining their wishes and naming a surrogate decision-maker—but even these patients went on to receive aggressive medical treatment in most cases. According to the SUPPORT researchers, the documents were "ineffectual in shaping care."

Another difficult aspect of dying today is the emotional toll. Psychological pain is difficult to measure or study, but interviews with doctors, nurses, families, and patients suggest that for a majority of people, dying is not only prolonged and needlessly painful, it is also lonely and frightening. In the hospital, patients are demeaned by the power and complexity of the institution and the technology therein, they are dehumanized by a web of tubes, wires, and intravenous lines, and they are invaded regularly by hospital staff who take blood samples and check monitors and medications at all hours of the day and night. Patients often become depressed and anxious, symptoms that are often left untreated. The trouble is, physical pain exacerbates psychological pain, and vice versa, so the patient is drawn into a downward spiral of deepening depression, distress, and pain.

Perhaps most disturbing of all, people who are dying are typically distanced, both physically and emotionally, from loved ones, who can't hurdle the physical intrusions of the hospital, and who often don't have any idea of how to help or what to do. They feel powerless and frightened in the face of death. They don't know how to offer their love, to say their good-byes, or to provide solace to a loved one who is dying, and especially one who is dying in such a way.

Patients are also isolated by denial and the deception of false hope—a deception that is fostered by doctors, family and friends, and sometimes by the patients themselves. Most people don't want to admit that death is near, talk about that process, or acknowledge the patient's feelings about what is happening. They simply don't want to believe that there isn't one last drug or one more procedure that might turn things around. Although lies and denial in the face of death have become particularly common and problematic recently, they have certainly existed before. In "The Death of Ivan Ilyich," Leo Tolstoy describes this deception:

> What tormented Ivan Ilyich most was the pretense, the lie, which for some reason they all kept up, that he was merely ill and not dying, and that he only need stay quiet and carry out the doctor's orders, and then some great change for the better would result. But he knew that whatever they might do nothing would come of it except still more agonizing suffering and death. And the pretense made him wretched: it tormented him that they refused to admit what they knew and he knew to be a fact, but persisted in lying to him concerning his terrible condition, and wanted him and forced him to be a party to the lie. . . . Many a time when they were playing their farce for his benefit he was within a hair's breadth of shouting at them: "Stop lying! You know, and I know, that I am dying. So do at least stop lying about it!" But he had never had the spirit to do it. The awful, terrible act of his dying was, he saw, reduced by those about him to the level of a fortuitous, disagreeable and rather indecent incident. . . . This falsity around and within him did more than anything else to poison Ivan Ilyich's last days.

This denied, medically managed death is clearly torturous for patients, but it is also horrible for family members and other loved ones, for they often miss the chance to say good-bye, to smooth out wrinkles in the relationship, and to give a final gift of support and love, a gift they often want desperately to bestow but don't know how.

A walk through almost any bookstore reveals that the vast majority of books written on death are not about death itself, but about grief, and I wonder, as I glance through the dozens of titles, if grief has become unusually burdensome for us in large part because our loved ones die so poorly. Because we aren't prepared for it, we haven't accepted the inevitability of death, and we haven't set a stage for death in which we can reminisce and begin to grieve and give the love that we need so badly to give. Many of us are left, instead, like Maureen, with unsettling memories and deep regrets. In the wake of death, we must shoulder not only an excessive amount of grief, but also guilt, anger, and bewilderment. How, despite all our best intentions, despite all our promises and legal papers, did it happen this way? What could we have done differently? And how, given this experience of death, as an agonizing and solitary exit, can we face the prospect of our own deaths and the deaths of others we love?

In his book *How We Die*, Dr. Sherwin B. Nuland writes, "Death belongs to the dying and to those who love them." Clearly, it should. But it doesn't. It belongs to doctors and hospitals and drug manufacturers and insurance programs and policy-makers, all of whom drive the direction of our care and treatment. They own our final days and months. They own our dying. They own it because, over the past several decades, we have turned it over to them. We have ceded control, and now we don't know enough about the process to redirect it or regain control over it.

It doesn't have to be this way. We can reclaim death. We have the power to change it, to make it ours again.

a matter of survival

efforts at reform have fallen short

The effort has already begun. We have tried to reclaim death, to make it better, to make it ours. We have touted the value of living wills and other legal documents that outline our wishes concerning end-of-life care. We have hailed the work of hospice programs and used their services in growing numbers. We have even toyed with the idea of allowing physicians to help dying patients kill themselves. Now a movement is afoot to train doctors in how to care for and counsel patients when the end is in sight. Obviously, all of this is important; better services and better training of doctors are desperately needed. But these efforts have not had the sort of impact one might expect, and they never will. Not by themselves.

The legal documents that people often think will protect them from a dreadful death have a woefully poor track record. These papers, known as advance directives, include two forms: a living will and a power of attorney for health care (also known as a "health care proxy"). A living will outlines a person's preferences for medical treatment at the end of life, typically stating that if the person is near death and has no reasonable hope of recovery, he or she does not want to be kept alive by "extraordinary" or "heroic" means. A power of attorney for health care authorizes some other person, usually a family member, to make medical decisions should the patient be unable to make such decisions for himself.

While advance directives have raised awareness and led to some broad changes, they have surprisingly little effect on how most people die today. They certainly don't do what most people expect them to do: protect them from a drawn-out, machine-operated death. In the SUPPORT study, researchers found that doctors typically didn't know about a patient's directives and that even when they did know of them, the doctor and patient failed to discuss what the patient wanted or how to carry out those wishes. Out of 4,804 patients, a mere 22 had directives that specifically addressed the use of life-sustaining treatment in the patient's current condition, and even in these cases, half the patients still received unwanted medical care.

Advance directives are ignored not because doctors are overzealous, or because hospitals don't care. They are ignored largely because a generic statement made in better times has little bearing on the complex and emotionally wrenching choices that arise when a life is in the balance.

A standard living will, for example, directs a physician to withhold or withdraw treatment that, in the typical words of the document, "serves only to prolong the process of my dying if I should be in an incurable or irreversible mental or physical condition with no reasonable expectation of recovery." But what does that really mean? If there is a slim chance that a person will get a little better, is that a "reasonable expectation"? If a person stands to regain some level of consciousness, but no other abilities, is that considered a "recovery"? Indeed, when is someone even considered to be "dying"? If a patient is in the early stages of a disease that will eventually be fatal, but maybe not for some time, is that person "dying"?

Even if the language were more precise, how is one to know what a person was thinking when he or she signed such a document? Did he mean that no life-sustaining treatments should be used at all, under any circumstances? If your father has heart disease and a stroke leaves him partially paralyzed, should he be given antibiotics to treat a life-threatening but treatable infection? If your wife has emphysema and has stated that she doesn't want to be put on a ventilator once death is near, does that mean that you shouldn't even try the intervention for a day to two, just to see if it might get her through a temporary crisis? Did your loved one consider a blood transfusion or dialysis to be an "extraordinary measure"? What was the signer's intention? Why did she want to avoid these treatments? What are you to do?

Because of this confusion, experts often say that a power of attorney, also known as a health care or medical proxy, is the form to have. But most people acting as proxies have only a vague idea of what their loved ones would want. All they know is that this person didn't want to be "kept alive" or didn't want "anything heroic." My own father, a doctor who dealt with dying patients all the time, offered this useful bit of guidance: "When I'm decrepit, take me out with the garbage."

Advance directives are absolutely worth having. They offer a layer of protection, legally documenting your wishes and tipping the scales when there is debate or confusion about what to do. But they cannot, by themselves, change the way we die.

Hospice programs, which would seem to be just what the doctor ordered, have not been wildly successful either. Hospices operate under the philosophy that death is a natural event and that at some point, rather than fighting vigorously to fend off death, all efforts should be focused on making the most of life—largely by keeping the person as comfortable and involved as possible. Hospice care is sometimes provided in a special hospice building or in a wing of a health-care facility, but usually it is offered within the patient's own home with the help of the family. Doctors and nurses focus on pain and symptom control, while social workers, counselors, clergy, and other staff members help patients meet any personal goals they might have, repair torn relationships, and find spiritual and psychological peace. Hospice workers also guide family members through the day-to-day work of caregiving and provide them with much-needed encouragement and counseling. (For more on hospice care, see pages 145–48.)

Yet, with all they have to offer, hospice programs serve only about 15 percent of the people who die each year—only a small fraction of those who could benefit from such services. Furthermore, those who hook up with a hospice typically do so very late in the game, on average within one month of dying, and often just days, or even hours, before death. At this point, patients are so sick that they cannot communicate or gain much from counseling, and pain has rooted itself so deeply that it is difficult if not impossible to treat successfully. This late in the process, all that hospice workers can do is provide what Carolyn Cassin, the former president of Hospice of Michigan, calls "brink-of-death care."

"At that point, we are literally managing the dying process. We are not managing the dying experience, which should take place over weeks and months, when a person can think and talk," she said. "It's a travesty. When you see it done right, when someone has the time to say good-bye, to leave whatever legacy they want. . . . It is not macabre and horrible. It's wonderful."

Physician-assisted suicide raises all sorts of fascinating legal, ethical, and medical issues, but when it comes down to it, few people want to kill themselves, even when they are terminally ill. We might think we would choose such an option, we might swear that we would take that route, but for most people, when they are standing on the edge of an abyss looking into the darkness below, a loud voice screams out, "Hang on!" even if the plan all along had been to jump.

Dr. Kathleen Foley, a neurologist at Memorial Sloan-Kettering Cancer Center who is one of the most widely respected authorities on end-of-life care, says that when patients ask her about suicide, she tells them, "I can help you live. I can allow you to die. But I can't give you a drug and say take it whenever you want. That's just not who I am." Hearing this, these patients stay with her. Even those who adamantly support physician-assisted suicide and have made plans to kill themselves don't leave in search of a willing doctor. "They are comforted by the fact that you say, 'I value your life. I don't mind taking care of you. You are not a terrible burden, or if you are a terrible burden, I'm still going to take care of you. I am not going to abandon you,' " Dr. Foley explains.

Experts in end-of-life care contend that if suicidal patients were treated for depression and offered comprehensive palliative care (which is aimed at comfort rather than cure), and if their families were given adequate support, the idea of suicide would be not only unpopular, but almost unimaginable. So while physician-assisted suicide is an intellectually absorbing proposal, if it were broadly legalized it would probably not affect the way the vast majority of us die.

Finally, there is improved doctor training, which means teaching doctors how to care, both physically and emotionally, for patients who are going to die. This effort holds the greatest promise, for if doctors were better guides, this trip would not be so torturous. Most doctors have no idea how to deal with dying patients and their families; they desperately need training and role models in this incredibly difficult aspect of the job. But even better trained doctors won't completely solve the problem.

The reasons this and other efforts can't drastically change the way we die are numerous. But one obstacle stands out above the others, an obstacle that must be addressed if we are ever going to find a more peaceful dying. That obstacle is us.

We can blame the doctors and the hospitals, the legal system and the insurance programs, but we, the patients and family members and loved ones, hold a great deal of sway in how we die. No matter what forms have been signed or promises made in advance; no matter what excellent guidance a doctor might offer; no matter what services are available, the fact is that when life and death decisions arise, most of us falter. We are not prepared to stop life-sustaining treatment; we are not ready to switch from hospital to hospice care; we are not open to hearing a doctor's dim prognosis, no matter how sensitively it is delivered.

Standing at the bedside of a loved one, we freeze up, unable to think clearly, to digest all that must be digested, and to do what we might even know in our hearts should be done. We never expected it to come to this, or for it to be like this. The choices are more complicated and the emotions more acute than we ever anticipated. We aren't sure what the patient was thinking when she signed her advance instructions. We don't feel that it is quite time for hospice care. We don't want to forgo some chance of survival, no matter how slim. And, in all honesty, we aren't ready to let go. With a loved one lying there, still warm to touch, the decisions are too monumental. Maybe a ventilator would be okay. Maybe dialysis isn't such a bad idea. Maybe resuscitation should be attempted. Maybe this person I love can hang on just a little bit longer because my heart is breaking into a zillion pieces and I don't want to let go. As one woman said when her husband lay in an intensive care unit with advanced cancer, severe infection, and respiratory failure, "He wouldn't want this, but I cannot bear to lose him."

In all our outrage over how miserably people die, we forget that we, the patients, but particularly the family members, play a difficult but decisive role in how each death occurs.

"We take our cues from the patients," says Dr. Michael Jacobs, a professor of medicine at Stanford Medical Center, repeating a line I have heard countless times. He leans back in his chair and offers a story that most doctors can repeat in one version or another. He had a patient, he says, a woman in her mid-thirties, who was diagnosed with metastatic colon cancer—the cancer had spread to other parts of her body and was considered fatal. "It was clear in the beginning to everyone involved that she wasn't going to be cured, but she and her husband didn't want to hear that at all," Dr. Jacobs said. The couple wanted to pursue treatment, any treatment. Even when the cancer had taken over the young woman's lungs, her liver, and other areas of her body, they continued to seek out specialists, aggressive procedures, experimental treatments, and alternative therapies. Just weeks before the woman died—her belly swollen, her appetite gone, her exhaustion visible, and her lungs laboring for each drop of air—her husband was investigating experimental gene therapy. Three days before she died they convinced an oncologist to start her on an extremely toxic experimental chemotherapy.

"For me to say, 'Listen, now, you're dying, and we must talk about the fact that you're dying. This is stupid for you to do this,' that's not my role," Dr. Jacobs says. "My role is to listen and to be as sensitive as I can be to the patient first, and to the family. This woman and her husband were of the mind-set that somehow she was going to be cured."

Perhaps there is something Dr. Jacobs could have done or said. Perhaps somewhere along this awful trip, there was some way that he could have helped them to see the futility of their efforts, the needless pain they were enduring. Or perhaps there is something he did say—some vague comment or hopeful aside—that led them to believe that they could still rescue this dwindling life. It's hard to say. The cues are subtle and the dance is complex. When the subject is terminal illness, people hear what they want to hear, and say things that aren't what they mean. The doctor, the patient, and the loved ones all play a role in this confusion. Clearly, this patient and her husband had definite ideas about how they wanted to handle her illness, and Dr. Jacobs was not in a position to force them to take another course. He had to respect their views, their needs, and their way of coping.

Dr. Kenneth Prager, chairman of the medical ethics committee at New York Presbyterian Hospital, gets annoyed when people place all the blame on doctors. "Of the cases referred to my hospital's medical ethics committee concerning inappropriate care of hopelessly ill patients, by far the greatest percentage involve situations in which the family or the patient, not the doctor, insists on heroic and costly treatments," he said. "If you were to walk around intensive care units and look at people who are—quote, unquote—kept alive inappropriately, you would find that nine times out of ten it is because the patient and family want it that way, not because the doctor does."

Walking around an intensive care unit as Dr. Prager had suggested I do, I came upon a semiconscious 85-year-old woman with a thick ventilator hose blocking her mouth, intravenous lines in her arm and chest, a blood pressure monitor on her finger, and assorted lines running under the sheets to her legs, crotch, and belly. Her eyes were closed. She did not move. A cardiac monitor overhead recorded the steady rhythm of what remained of her life: *beep . . . beep . . . beep . . . beep . . . beep.* A nurse outlined her medical history for me. She was old and weak, with numerous organs in decline—heart, lungs, kidneys. She had been brought in initially because of massive internal bleeding, and then, having sucked blood into her lungs, she was treated for pneumonia. With that attended to, she was now being treated, quite frankly, for death. That is, all of her systems were failing.

It is not difficult to see how one thing had led to the next, but why was she still here receiving all this invasive care? Why didn't her family and the doctor let her go? The nurse shrugged. "Her daughter said, 'I don't want to hear about anything bad. I want you to do what you can to fix her.' So we do a little of this and a little of that. We can keep people alive, but we can't necessarily make them better."

We think this won't happen to us, that we wouldn't do that to our loved ones or that they wouldn't do it to us. We know better. But when we are there ourselves, the story often doesn't play out according to our plans. Quite often, even patients and families who have sworn that they wouldn't accept invasive care end up getting it simply because when it is time to say stop they aren't ready to do so, they don't know how to do so, or they don't see it as an option.

"If people have never been through an experience of someone dying, then they don't have a clue about any of these things. Not a clue," says Dr. Foley. "Even the most intelligent people say they never had a clue what was going on, never caught on. One, they never knew the person was dying even though the signs were all around them. Then, when they were dying, they didn't know what to say, what to do, they didn't know how to feel. They were just numb, and then it was over."

John McGuirk is a lawyer who has drafted hundreds of advance directives for clients. He thought he understood what the legal papers and the issues they cover were all about. He thought so, until his own father lay in an intensive care unit, "wired," as he puts it. "I walked past his room. I didn't even recognize him. He looked like this ancient man. He had tubes all around him. He weighed about 90 pounds."

It wasn't clear what was wrong with him, but John and his siblings knew that their father was dying. And yet, they didn't know. They weren't certain. "The problem is, it's not all that defined, and things happen quickly," John explains. "It's not black and white. No one said he was terminal, but we were thinking it. In your heart of hearts you know. But you're not prepared. . . . Maybe if I'd known more about what 'life-sustaining treatments' were. . . . The whole thing is shocking."

Joann Owen has stood in that place too. In 1984, Joann's mother, Violet, had surgery to remove a second brain tumor, and in the years that followed the procedure she repeatedly told her family that if anything were to happen, she did not want to endure "that sort of thing" again. "She would say, 'I'm tired. I've had enough. If anything else comes up, I don't want any more,' " Joann said. Violet never signed an advance directive, but her family felt that her wishes were clear. Then one afternoon, Violet went to the emergency room because she didn't feel well and her heart was beating rapidly. She stayed in the hospital for a few days while the doctors did some tests, and during that time she had a heart attack. Faced with a medical emergency and no clear instructions on what to do, the doctor put her on life support in the intensive care unit. She remained there, semicomatose, for a week, until she died. To this day, her daughter is pained by the memories.

In the ICU, Joann said, there was no room for intimacy or conversation and physical contact was all but impossible. During the rare moments when her mother was alert, she was alarmed to find herself in the hospital. "Because of all the tubes and this and that, you feel like you can't physically help, and it's hard to stroke someone or be near them. And you can't even imagine saying good-bye because it's like they are not even there. You're an observer. It was the equivalent of being at a wake. Everyone is just sitting there, marking time. It's like a death watch. I look back and wonder, 'What were we thinking? What happened here?' " Joann laments, "but the whole thing just snowballed."

At 78, Violet Owen had endured heart problems for some time, but for whatever reasons, her heart was not of primary concern. "I think she understood that we wouldn't do anything extraordinary, but I think she was thinking in terms of an operation. She was thinking in terms of her brain surgery. I don't know. She didn't ever spell it out," Joann said. "She had had angina for years, but that wasn't what we considered to be her problem."

If anyone had ever talked with Violet about what she meant by "nothing extraordinary," and "I've had enough," and then had discussed her wishes with the doctor, perhaps he would have known not to intubate her. Had the family known more about the medical system and the options available and what their mother wanted and what she didn't want, perhaps they would have asked that the ventilator be removed so that her dying would not be prolonged and so that they could say good-bye to her in peace. But little was known or discussed ahead of time. They weren't prepared to handle this moment, and so they saw no alternatives and made no decisions.

"We assumed we were pretty savvy. We felt that we knew what was going on. But we were stunned," Joann said. "Every one of us kept saying, 'Why are they doing this? Why can't we stop this?' Not one of us thought that we as individuals could stop it."

*   *   *

The point is, we die tethered to machines and enveloped by pain not simply because doctors aren't trained and palliative services are limited, but also because we, the patients and families, are simply not prepared to, or in some cases are not willing to, talk about death, much less allow it to happen. We acknowledge the horrible deaths of others and say that we want something else for ourselves and our loved ones, but then we blindly follow the same arduous path. We follow that path because it is there, it is well-worn, it is routine. We follow it because most of us don't know of any other path. And we follow it because when death draws near we are stymied by grief, disbelief, and ignorance. In a state of total devastation, we cannot begin to accept that someone we love is dying; we certainly cannot take action that will allow that process to happen.

This response is not all that surprising. Millions of years of evolution have instilled in humans a tremendously powerful—and at most times, very useful—instinct to live. We are programmed to keep fighting and screaming for help even when the saber-toothed tiger has us securely in its jaws. If we are on the sidelines and not running for our own lives, we wildly hurl any sticks and rocks that we can find at the beast. We are built to survive and to keep our loved ones alive. It is in our chemistry, in the core of our being. We don't want death to happen under any circumstances. In the past, we struggled and either we escaped or the tiger had a tasty meal; we survived the fever or we died. Nature called the shots and people knew how to respond. But all that has changed.

Over the past century—and especially in the past couple of decades—two things have happened. One, medicine has presented us with choices that we never had before, choices about when we will die and how we will die. Two, because it now usually takes place in an institution staffed with professionals instead of in the home, we have lost our familiarity with death and so we don't know the rituals and behaviors that should accompany it anymore.

These recent developments have put us to a bizarre test. Our most primal instincts tell us to fight to stay alive and to keep those we love alive; and yet, in this modern world we are supposed to make a carefully thought out decision about whether or not to allow death to happen, and, in many cases, when and how to let it happen. We are expected to say, "All right, we will allow this death to occur. We will skip this treatment or stop that treatment, and let this person we love depart from this world and from our lives." Unless there's been a fair amount of forethought and experience, it is extremely difficult to do such a thing. Unless we are ready, and truly determined, our instincts will almost always win out, or we will simply look on with horror and, by virtue of making no decision, continue to press on toward the ending we dread.

And so, rather than using medicine's new powers to our benefit— to ease the pain of death or to buy a little time when there is something important left to do—we let them be used to our detriment because not just the doctors, but we ourselves, are distanced from the reality of death and naïve about the decisions we must make at the end.

mere immortals

death has become a stranger

We react instinctively, and often poorly, when death approaches largely because we don't know death anymore. We don't see it and we rarely talk about it. Sure, we see more than our share of dead bodies, which are shown graphically on the front pages of newspapers and on television—bodies shot by gunmen, crushed by debris, or blown to pieces by bombs—and we see actors playing dying patients, but we rarely witness the process of dying as it routinely occurs. Most of us reach our thirties or forties without ever having seen a death or helped someone through a terminal illness. We may not have even heard about anyone's death in any great detail—the gradual decline, the fear, the treatments, the pain, or the intimacy that can occur in the final stage of life.

And so, while we know that death happens, we don't quite believe that it will happen to us, or to those we love—not in the foreseeable future anyway. We also don't have any vision of what we would do if it were to happen. We say that we wouldn't want to be "kept alive," but do we know exactly what life support is, and when it is used, how it might be stopped, or whether it can be refused? Do we have any idea what we might do for a loved one who is gasping for air but does not want to be "hooked to machines"?

The irony is that death has become unfamiliar territory just when there is so much more that we need to know about it. Advances in medicine have complicated death. We need to be savvy, and instead we have become less experienced and less knowledgeable about death than previous generations were.

Once upon a time people knew death. It was never welcome, of course, but throughout most of history it was at least familiar. People grew up seeing parents, children, spouses, friends, and neighbors die. They knew how death occurred, what to expect, and how to behave in the face of it. They knew this because people died at a relatively young age, they died quickly, and they died quite publicly.

The late French historian Philippe Ariès described death in the early part of the 20th century like this: a person, young or old, would become acutely ill with some infectious disease, such as influenza, pneumonia, or tuberculosis, and would die within two or three weeks. During those weeks of illness, the person would be at home under the care of family, friends, neighbors, and often some spiritual guide, such as a priest. As death approached, the bedroom shutters were pulled closed, candles were lit, and perhaps holy water was sprinkled. After the death, an announcement was posted on the front of the house, and the doors were left open to admit visitors, who came in droves. Everyone attended the funeral, and then for weeks afterward people continued to visit the cemetery and the family. "It was not only an individual who was disappearing, but society itself that had been wounded and that had to be healed," Ariès wrote in his book *The Hour of Our Death.*

Over the past hundred years, and particularly in the last few decades, death has become an increasingly private and individual act. Most notably in America, the care of dying people has passed from the community to the family and then, in recent decades, to hospitals, nursing homes, and other institutions. This shift occurred for many reasons, foremost among them the rapid changes in medicine.

At one time hospitals discharged people as soon as they became incurable because there was little doctors could do for them beyond offering a little comfort and compassion. Early in the 20th century, narcotic painkillers were available without a prescription, so doctors were not needed even for that. People who died in a hospital were there either because they were poor or because they had no family. Then medicine began to make enormous strides, developing ways to fight deadly infections, recharge failing hearts, transplant sickly organs, and refuel the body with blood and oxygen. Suddenly doctors had an arsenal of treatments to offer critically ill patients. Their care was no longer something simple and spiritual, but something prolonged and complex, something that had to be done in a hospital. In 1950, half of all deaths in America occurred in institutions, mostly hospitals. Today that figure is up to nearly 80 percent.

Not only did death disappear into the hospital, it has disappeared *within* the hospital. In all the time I have spent in hospitals, as a child following behind my physician father, as a medical reporter trailing a story, as an author researching books, as a patient, and as a visitor, I don't believe I have ever seen a dead patient. Come to think of it, I can't recall having seen a gathering of grief-stricken survivors either. Certainly people die along these hallways. They die here all the time. So where are they?

It turns out that when a patient dies in a modern American hospital, the door is closed immediately or the curtains are drawn, and the staff goes quickly and quietly into action. The body is wrapped in plastic and laid in a special stretcher sent from the morgue. It is placed in a sling or box that hangs beneath the metal frame of a gurney, and then a cloth is laid over the top so that, to the untrained eye, the vehicle appears to be an empty gurney or a laundry cart. The cart is wheeled down to a service elevator or, in smaller hospitals, to the regular elevators after staff members have made sure that the coast is clear and that no members of the public are loitering in the hallway. Once in the morgue, bodies are picked up at a rear entrance of the hospital by undertakers driving unmarked vans or station wagons. Meanwhile, grieving family members, if they happen to be around, are whisked into a private family room where they can grieve without being noticed, or they are taken to the morgue if they wish to see the body. No one in the hospital is reminded that death occurs here, or that it occurs at all for that matter.

The clandestine nature of death in American hospitals first became apparent to me about 20 years ago when I was traveling in China, a kid with a backpack trying to learn about the world. Somewhere around Shanghai my finger became swollen and green with infection, so I found my way to a local hospital and was led to a doctor who ordered a series of shots. As I walked back down the hallway, trying to remember how to get to the front door and wondering what had just been injected into my rear end, I heard a scream. Then I heard several screams, and then a chorus of shrieking and wailing.

As I came around the corner I saw about a dozen people, jammed in the doorway of a room, sobbing and holding each other and carrying on. In the room were six beds, each one occupied by a patient. One of the patients was dead. The other five patients lay calmly, watching the commotion in silence. A nurse stood by, allowing this scene to continue.

I walked away, stunned. I was surprised because in the months that I had been in China I had found people to be reserved, and I was surprised because I had never seen such a thing—not anything even remotely like it—in a Western hospital. Maybe that is just as well. But maybe it's not.

a funeral of flowers

As death was moved into institutions and hidden behind doors, it was further concealed from the public eye by the rise of the funeral industry, which profited from our growing discomfort with death. Once upon a time, Aunt Mary's dead body would have been cleaned, clipped, combed, and dressed by family members, viewed by most of the community, and laid out in a homemade pine box to be buried. The cost in today's dollars: a couple of hundred bucks, if that, because the family or a local carpenter built the casket and neighbors brought the food. Then, after several days of viewings and visitors and services, the family would begin a period of public grieving that lasted weeks or months.

Today, Aunt Mary is zipped up in a bag and whisked out the door. A team of morticians, makeup artists, caterers, and florists, who don't know the patient or family, go to work hiding any sign of illness or death. Bodies are often embalmed (a process in which blood and other bodily fluids are replaced with preservatives), even though this is rarely necessary, and then they are beautified—plumped and waxed and airbrushed, given new hair, new lips, new teeth, new skin color—to make them look "lifelike" and give them a "natural" glow. They are bedded in cushioned caskets made of pine, oak, rolled steel, or copper bronze (one of hand-polished African mahogany costs $10,000), lined with velvet, velour, or twill, and covered with an abundance of flowers. To further the illusion of eternal existence and make the burial more palatable (and more expensive) for the survivors, the casket can be sealed and placed in a vault of galvanized steel. This is done under the pretense of protecting the body—from decay, worms, gophers, air, moisture—although nothing prevents the body from decomposing. For those who still can't deal with death, there are other options outside the realm of the funeral home, such as cryonic freezing or mummification ("Keeps you looking healthy and robust for millennia" boasts one ad).

The funeral is then packaged into a single day, or at most a few days, of services and social gathering. Black mourning clothes are either not worn or are worn only briefly, and the fact that someone has died is barely mentioned. Overt grief is seen as morbid or hysterical; survivors are urged to get on with life as quickly as possible. The cost of the funeral: $4,000 and up.

This is all part of the $7 billion funeral industry. We used to be able to sidestep some of the carnival by opting for cremation (or maybe we were simply furthering the illusion that nothing had happened), but even cremation isn't necessarily simple anymore. Funeral directors, realizing they are losing money on caskets, now offer products aimed at what are called "cremains." You can buy solid bronze urns or custom-designed urns that come shaped like cowboy boots, golf club bags, hunting trophies—you name it. You can buy clusters of urns so each loved one can have their own handful of ashes, or cremation jewelry in case you want to carry a sprinkle in a locket. You can put your loved one in a pricey mausoleum vault built specially for urns or pay to scatter your loved one's ashes around in a special cemetery garden.

All of this stands in sharp contrast to the funeral of Duane Whelan, a lawyer from my hometown. Duane was a big man and very handsome, with a ruddy complexion and a mop of unruly white hair. He went to church every Sunday and sailed whenever he got the chance, but more than anything else, Duane was a family man who raised 12 children of his own and kept in very close contact with his siblings and their children.

When Duane died, at the age of 76, several of his children drove to a nearby funeral parlor to pick out a casket. They walked up and down the aisles, looking at the simple and the ornate. They pondered the soft cushions and spring mattresses. They ran their fingers along the velvet and crepe liners. They examined the different woods and metals, the cherry, the poplar, the copper, and the silver. But in the end, they simply could not pick anything out. None of the caskets seemed right. Not for Duane. Not for their dad. "It felt so distant, looking at these things that had no connection at all to my father," his son Peter recalls.

So Peter and his brothers left the funeral home and drove over to the local lumberyard. There, they walked through the tall storehouses, taking in the scent of fresh-cut wood and feeling the smooth grain of the planks. After some time, they selected several long, broad pieces of pine and some crown molding, loaded it in the back of Peter's truck, and headed home.

That afternoon, assorted members of the family—children, grandchildren, in-laws, nieces, and nephews—gathered to build Duane's final resting place. It was early October, but the autumn air was still warm, so they worked outside, sawing, hammering, shaping, and measuring, throughout the day and into the night. One A.M. Two A.M. Three A.M. The hours passed without notice. This was a mission of love. Sleep was not an issue. They built the interior frame like the inside of a sailboat, a place where Duane had always been happy. They designed a recessed panel for the top of the casket. They screwed on hand-forged hinges of shiny brass that one son had bought in India many years ago, attached six handles of heavy rope to be used for carrying, and then lined the interior with a soft black blanket that had been given to Duane and his wife as a gift some years earlier. With the smell of sawdust and varnish in the cool night air, the family talked as they worked, reminiscing about Duane and the years they had had with him. Sometimes, while they talked, they laughed. Sometimes, they wept. Either way, it felt good.

"It was a wonderful experience," Peter says. "I can't really explain it. It gave us a focus and a whole different feeling to the funeral. It gave the family a connection to the process because everyone had a part in it."

Unfortunately, this is far from the norm. In fact, people are often stunned, and even put off, by the idea of such personal involvement in a funeral and such open acknowledgment of grief. This is not our way anymore. Death has been removed from our sight and replaced with a final display of lilies.

Oddly enough, rather than making death more manageable, this quarantining of death has made it that much more difficult. It has distanced us from the process and, in doing so, has turned death into an unknown, unseen and, therefore, more frightening prospect. It has stripped us of experience and wisdom, and stolen from us the rituals and the intimacy that, while deeply painful, used to make death and the ensuing grief more bearable.

illusion of immortality

As we have been increasingly insulated from death, we have also been bombarded by suggestions that we are, to some extent, immune from it. Almost daily we hear about medical breakthroughs, miraculous recoveries, foods and hormones and chemicals that can fend off disease, potions and regimes that will keep us young. The newspapers, self-help books, and infomercials insist that we can win the battle against life-threatening diseases, that we can slow the aging process, and that we can extend our lives significantly, if not indefinitely. This feeling of immunity, this sneaking suspicion that we can control our lives as well as our demise, has further distanced us from death, made us that much more naïve about the dying process, and fooled us in such a way that we are often completely shocked when death comes.

Larry and Candy Wood of California, who were featured in a *New York Times Magazine* article, are shining examples of this preoccupation with extending life. The Woods spend most of their time trying to have more time. Lean and muscular, they exercise obsessively, don't touch alcohol or tobacco, and gulp down or inject everything from the relatively mundane (melatonin, vitamins, beta-carotene) to the unpronounceable (glutathione, manganese picolinate, L-Ornithine). Soon, they contend, scientists will know how to extend life and they don't want to kick off before that ship comes in.

The Woods are part of a rapidly growing subculture of "immortalists," people who believe that life can be preserved almost indefinitely, in one form or another. Life Extensionists, like the Woods, think life can be preserved as we now know it, both a mind and a body, while other immortalists are focused on saving just one piece of the pie. Some want to preserve the body, mummified or frozen, until it can be revived when science has found the key of life. Some are socking away a complete set of their own DNA in the hope of becoming whole again at a later date. Still others contend that the intellect, the ego, the soul can be made eternal. Through "uploading" or "cybernetic immortality," they believe that people will be able to transfer all their thoughts, memories, desires, impulses, biases— everything, pretty much, that makes them who they are—onto a computer. Then, according to the Principia Cybernetica Web site, "if at a certain stage the biological individual of this symbiotic couple would die, the computational part might carry on as if nothing had happened." In other words, your body would be kaput, but the cyber-you could go on, teaching your children, finishing your book, e-mailing your friends.

All of this may be a bit on the fringe, but it's not as far out as you might think. A number of reputable scientists now insist that senescence is not as immutable as we once thought, and that one day, probably one day not all that far off, the human life span will be extended significantly, perhaps even doubled. They hold up as their proof several recent discoveries: with a few genetic alterations, scientists have doubled the life span of worms, fruit flies, and mice, and allowed them to live those extra years in exuberant health; scientists have pinpointed a genetic flaw that causes yeast to grow old quickly and humans to age prematurely; researchers have known for some time that a low-calorie diet extends the lives of mice significantly; and they have discovered and isolated "immortal" human cells, known as embryonic stem cells, which grow and divide indefinitely.

Coupled with this work on senescence are a host of medical discoveries—new cancer treatments, gene therapies, clot-clearing drugs, and the like—each aimed at defeating a particular life-threatening illness. We hear about them almost every day. And indeed, they are awesome and inspiring. Breakthroughs in medicine, even when they are made only in petri dishes, add to the belief that death can be defeated, or at least that death from the usual causes can be prevented. We just have to hang on until the final trials are finished and the FDA approvals are in place.

Two other trends have also altered our sensibility about death. The first, a hot topic, is prevention. Dozens of new studies insist that we can fend off age and disease by the way we live. We simply need to eat five servings of fruits and vegetables a day; exercise regularly, but not too strenuously; have one glass of wine, but not two, each day; toss out our cigarettes; pray; consume vitamins; buckle our seat belts; avoid fat, salt, cholesterol, charred food, pesticides, bovine hormones and anything we can't pronounce; take hormones, antioxidants, and a lot of stuff we can't pronounce; trust alternative medicine; reduce stress; eat garlic; and stay away from people who haven't tossed out their cigarettes.

Don't get me wrong. These are good things to do. In fact, they are great things to do. It's just that we have become so fixated on life-prolonging habits and so strident in our desire for—indeed, our right to—self-determination, that we have gained a false sense of control over death. We feel that if we live right, we'll live long; if we live wrong, we'll die early. If only it were that simple. These things may give us a little more life, or a little more energy, but they won't change the inevitable. We will die, no matter how much broccoli we devour.

The second trend that has altered our thinking about death is a change in our attitudes about old age. Old age used to be revered and respected, but today it is viewed with full-blown disdain. Gathering years is nothing to be proud of; rather, it is something to hide. Forget the glory of age; the fountain of youth is what we are after. We work fervently to get rid of wrinkles, white hairs, extra folds. More creams, surgery, implants, injections, lifts, peels, suctions, skin smoothers, and hair dyes. The American Academy of Anti-Aging Medicine claims, complete with uppercase letters, that "Aging is NOT inevitable," and the Longevity Institute in Arizona, which offers biomarker analysis, matrix profiles, and hormone therapy, states, with ample exclamation points, "Remember—Aging is a Treatable Condition!!!" According to a recent article in *The Washington Post*, the sales of products touting "age-defying" or "anti-aging" properties went from $325 million in the mid-1990s to a whopping $3.6 billion by the end of the century. You want to get rid of wrinkles? There are now more than 1,700 anti-wrinkle creams available to choose from.

Even those who accept old age as a fact of life are convincing us that we don't have to grow old in the traditional way; we can grow old with spark and spunk and zip. We can live "fully." We can age "successfully." We can travel and read and learn and love and dance along beaches and jump over tennis nets. We don't have to sit in wheelchairs, growing weaker and blinder and denser. We have the power to stay young, in appearance and action. This is the ethos of our times.

As seductive as all of this is, most of us accept, intellectually at least, that life is finite, that we probably won't see 100, and that Jeanne Calment, the French woman who lived to be 122, was a rare bird. Many might even argue that they don't want to double their life spans; that 75 or 80 years is ample time on this planet. It is overcrowded anyway.

And yet, with all this talk of longevity and medical triumphs and successful aging in the air, one can't help wondering. The message that we can win the battle, or at least put up a very good fight, is hard to ignore. It is loud and alluring, and it is always there, in the background of our lives, teasing us, tempting us, baiting us. How can we disregard it? We know that people die, but when it happens, a little voice in us asks: What did he do to deserve it? Did he smoke? Did he drink? Did he live near a nuclear power plant? Did he eat too many Twinkies? What did he do that we don't do or could avoid doing? We know that death happens, but maybe it is not a random occurrence or strike of God; maybe it is, after all, something we can control.

Throughout history, death has loomed over life, shaping religions, philosophies, cultures, and everyday practices. But today, it doesn't loom. We don't ruminate over death and the meaning of life. Instead, we talk almost incessantly about how to prolong a youthful and energetic life. We Americans are particularly prone to this notion that we can control death. As someone once said, "Americans don't die; they underachieve."

We are not stupid. We are victims of our culture, of the news and hype that surrounds us each and every day. All the things that once prepared us for death—regular experience with illness and death, public grief and mourning, a culture and philosophy of death, interaction with the elderly, as well as the visibility of our own aging—are virtually gone from our lives. Instead, we are tempted daily by that perfect apple, by promises of youth and immortality.

And so it is in this state, with little knowledge of death, a blind faith in medicine, and a strong sense of personal control over life, that we enter the doctor's office and the realm of terminal illness, and begin making decisions about how we and our loved ones will die. It is no wonder that we have trouble accepting the reality of death, managing death once it arrives, or making sense of it once it has happened.

a portrait of death

a look at life's end

Throughout a good part of history, and even today in many cultures, people not only knew death, they studied it. They thought about it and prepared for it, learning well in advance how to die and how to help others die. During the 15th century, after printmakers developed a way to produce woodcuts cheaply and pictures could be distributed widely, it became common to study *ars moriendi*, the art of dying. At the time, people had little control over death or its physical symptoms, so the art of dying was largely religious. According to the elaborate pictures detailed in the woodcuts, in the last hour of life the devil and his army would make a final rush for the soul, tempting it with an abundance of evils: materialism, despair, pride, arrogance, loss of faith, and the like. Those who learned *ars bene moriendi*, the art of dying well, knew how to enlist the help of angels and saints in resisting the magnetic pull of the devil. They knew how to embrace a humility and peace that would please God, thereby securing for themselves a ticket to heaven instead of hell.

Since Judgment Day is not a pressing concern for the majority of people today, and we now have all sorts of ways to manipulate death, we need to rethink the art of dying well and come up with a new description that suits the times. If we don't want to die alone in a hospital hooked to machines, if we don't want to die in pain after a series of brutal and pointless medical treatments, how *do* we want to die? What would be acceptable, peaceful, and for some of us even meaningful? What do we consider to be "a good death"? What should we strive for, for ourselves and for our loved ones?

Before we do any of this, however, we need to understand how people really die today. Where are they and what are they up against? Unfortunately, Hollywood has given us a lasting impression of a good death: a beautiful young woman—for some reason it is always a woman—is lying in an expansive, pillowy bed, her makeup just so. A doctor, nurse, or loved one stands in attendance. There is a tender, knowing look, some parting words, and then the eyes gently close, the body goes limp, and it is over.

Although filmmakers have added the emergency room death to their repertoire—a huddle of frantic doctors and nurses yelling out for drugs and heart rates and clamps—the standard Hollywood death scene has changed little over the years. In the movie *Terms of Endearment*, Debra Winger plays Emma Horton, a young mother who dies of breast cancer. Few deaths are as difficult and labored as the death of a mother who leaves behind young children, for her work is not done. She is hard-pressed to accept death or to find any sort of ease or peace in dying.

In the movie version of this sorrowful death, when the doctor says that the lump is malignant, Emma cries. Everyone cries. But after some anguish and some humor and one failed attempt at a cure with drugs, everyone accepts openly that she is going to die. She moves into a large, private hospital room—cozy quilt, oil paintings, fresh flowers, picture windows, framed photos—where she is free of machines or tubes and is strong enough to get herself from bed to chair and back again. She has a warm but matter-of-fact talk with her husband about who will raise the children (the loving dad says calmly that he'll miss them, but agrees that Emma's mother will take them), and then Emma says a brief, misty good-bye to her small children. Finally, we see the husband and Emma's mother slumped in chairs in the hospital room. The husband is sleeping soundly, the mother is clenched in silent grief. Emma looks tired and pale, but her hair is thick, her body young, and her mind clear. Except for what appears to be a small intravenous drip there is no sign of hospital mechanics or medical intrusion. She turns toward her mother with a knowing look, waves a few fingers slowly good-bye, and then closes her eyes to die. A nurse in a starched white outfit walks in, takes her pulse, and announces that she is gone.

Any attempt to reclaim death or to define what it is that we want, must start with an understanding of what death is—and what it isn't. And it isn't *Terms of Endearment*. If we picture ourselves or our loved ones drifting gently off like Sleeping Beauty we will always feel that we have failed. If we picture doctors jump-starting a fading heart or discovering a new therapy at the last minute, bringing someone miraculously back not only to life, but to a meaningful and worthwhile life, we will be deeply disappointed.

Death can follow a hundred different routes. It can happen suddenly from a heart attack, or violently during an accident, but more often than not, it comes after an extended illness, a battery of tests and invasive procedures, numerous hospitalizations, endless discussions and decisions about treatment, periods of decline and periods of improvement, and the untold amounts of disbelief, denial, and pain. In the end, most people are in a hospital or nursing home; a lucky few die at home. Some are amid friends and family; many are alone.

Wherever they are, most people who are near death appear diminished, as if they have lost not only weight but height as well; they are shrunken from their previous size and stature. Their hair may be thin, their skin pale, almost translucent, and their appetites meager or gone. People tend to be extremely tired when they are dying, drifting in and out of sleep, too weak to lift an arm or to hold a conversation. About half of dying people are unconscious most of the time, while others are likely to have periods of confusion. Some are anxious, many are surprisingly peaceful. Most people who are close to death are incontinent or too weak to get on a commode, so they are hooked to catheters or wrapped in diapers. Some are disfigured by illness or surgery. Some receive oxygen through a thin tube feeding into the nose. In an institution, especially in an intensive care unit, patients may be connected to an array of machinery, such as ventilators, heart monitors, blood pressure monitors, intravenous equipment, defibrillators, catheters, feeding tubes, and dialysis machines.

Although pain can be eliminated or made bearable in virtually every case, most people do not receive good comfort care. They may moan wearily or cry out when touched, or they might struggle with symptoms such as nausea, strained breathing, depression, and bed sores. Even those who receive good care typically suffer during their illness and treatments, before they are at the point of getting palliative care, and then during the intervals when pain medications must be adjusted.

It is impossible to predict exactly when someone will die. People with heart or lung disease can be quite ill for an extended period and then die relatively suddenly. Sometimes people who seem close to death hang on for weeks or months, while others die just as they have acquired new strength or clarity. Either way it is confusing and upsetting for families. In most cases, however, especially in cases of terminal cancer, people fade gradually and there are signs that death is imminent. In the last day or two of life, they often float in and out of consciousness, their toes and fingers become cool, and their breathing becomes irregular. Then, as the throat muscle relaxes and secretions collect, a person's breathing may become noisy—a sound referred to as a death rattle—which is not uncomfortable for the patient, but can upset families. Death itself may be anticlimactic; the person simply stops breathing. Sometimes a person will look as though he is gasping for air or writhing in agony, but in most cases this is not because he is suffering; it is simply the result of muscles contracting involuntarily.

All of this may sound horrible, and the plain truth is that aside from suddenly collapsing dead on the 18th hole, there is no easy way out of this world. It takes nine months and a lot of hard pushing to get people into it, and it usually takes at least that much effort to get them out. Dying is difficult work. It involves pain and grief, and it would be pure folly to imagine that it didn't or that we could avoid suffering altogether. When we talk about "dying well" or "a good death," we have to remember that no death is truly "good"; we are always talking about making the best of a difficult, inevitable, and very human event.

It is also important to understand that what we see at a glance can be deceptive and our impressions of suffering may be misplaced. If you peek into the room of a dying person without having any idea of what is truly happening there, you may jump back in horror and mutter to yourself, "No way, not for me. I'll kill myself first!" But that may be because you have averted your gaze before you had a chance to fully understand what is happening.

One room in particular comes to mind. It is an airy, sunny room in a large house at the end of a rural cul-de-sac. There is a hospital bed in the corner and in it lie the skeletal remains of a man. He is ashen and weak. He drools from what remains of his mouth. Cancer has eroded his jaw, and his tongue is so swollen that he can't close his lips. A large bandage on his neck covers an area where a tumor has pushed its way through his skin. The hospice nurse worries that the tumor could grow into his carotid artery, which would then spew like a geyser, leaving him to die in a rainstorm of his own blood— thus the pile of dark towels in the corner. A tube leads from his nose down the hall to a humming machine that concentrates the oxygen in the air for him. When he speaks, his words are so quiet and garbled that they are incomprehensible to anyone but the hospice workers and the man's children.

His children, yes, they are there too, all grown up. A daughter sits by his side, looking tenderly at him, holding his hand and stroking his arm. A son sits at the end of the bed with his niece who is squealing, delighted by her uncle's antics.

Many years ago this man's children left him because of his drinking, because of his behavior. Now they are back, reconciled, caring, tending to him daily. They are back because he is their father, because despite any mistakes he made in the past he is a good man, and because they do not want to lose him. Their devotion is clear, and the longer I stay in this room, the more I feel its presence. I feel it until, after some time, I hardly see the disease and disfigurement anymore. Instead I see a daughter's forgiveness, a son's love, and enormous pride in the care they are giving their father. I see sadness for what they are losing, but also solace in what they have created before it was too late. I see a man who, despite what is happening to his body, is rich, very rich, in heart and soul.

As I am taking all of this in, a hospice social worker takes the man's hand in hers and bends over him. He is very close to death—in fact, he will be gone within 24 hours. I can't hear all of her words, but I can see his face relaxing in the sweet rhythm of her voice. "Rest, just rest," she whispers softly. As she looks at him, her eyes reveal such tenderness and caring that it is clear that she, too, has come under the spell of this man and all that is happening in this room.

His illness is a wretched one and I have no doubt that he has suffered enormously along the way. But the ghastliness of his appearance now, on the verge of death, in no way reflects what his dying is about. In the past eight months, with the help of the local hospice, he has spent innumerable hours tending to his garden. He has cooked Thanksgiving dinner for his family, he has relished Christmas morning with his grandchildren, and he has organized a family Easter egg hunt. He has not only mended his damaged relationships with his children, he has developed a deep bond with them. He has gotten to know his grandchildren and they have gotten to know him. He is reasonably comfortable now and although, from what I can tell, he has spent little of his life in peace, he now has a great deal of it. His family, while grieving, have been given a chance to forgive him, get to know him, love him, and say good-bye to him. No one would choose to have throat cancer. No one would choose to have their children leave them. But for someone who has had such a life, this dying is quite a sight to behold.

Death is the one instance in which a picture does not say a thousand words, for in death it is not the disability or disfigurement but the caresses, the gazes, the meticulous physical tending, the spiritual discoveries, and the private emotions—spoken and unspoken—that truly convey what is happening. In the end, it is not the act of dying, but all those final moments of living, that are truly important.

To understand just how varied the roads to death can be, and what death is beyond the frightening facade, allow me to lead you into a few more rooms, a few more lives, starting with Betty Holden, who has lost both her husband and her father. Two deaths, very different from one another.

Betty's father, whom she absolutely adored, was in his early seventies when he was diagnosed with cancer of the gallbladder. Surgery to remove the tumor revealed that the cancer had spread throughout his body. He was told he had only months to live, and was sent home without further ado to live out his final days. "At first Dad rebelled," Betty recalls. "He said, 'If I can't live a high-quality life, I'm going to shoot myself.' But that didn't last too long."

George Walker was a wealthy man who ran an investment brokerage company. He was geared to a competitive world, was tough in business, and had very high standards and expectations for himself and those around him. When he was faced with death, another powerful facet of the man surfaced.

"He had, I'll call it, a spiritual transformation," Betty says. "Dad was a tough man and he made a lot of people angry and stepped on a lot of toes. He was very, very strong. But he walked back through all of his life. He went through it and probably suffered through it. . . . Then his whole countenance of being changed. He became very sweet and tender. His face changed. Of course he got thinner because he wasn't taking much food, but his face became a very sweet, gentle, beautiful face. I would say tenderness and gentleness came into his being."

While he had always supported the local church and claimed to be religious, he became truly spiritual in his dying, Betty says. He met privately with a minister each day for about an hour, and when his grandchildren visited they would gather around his bed to pray with him, a ritual he cherished. His new devotion did not spring from fear, but rather from a new appreciation and understanding of life and death. "The minister said he'd never seen a person prepare himself for death as beautifully as my father had," Betty says.

"He was very open to talking about it, which was wonderful. His friends would call and Dad would say, 'Well, have you heard I've got cancer and they've given me about three months to live?' and then there he'd be off talking, talking, talking. It put everyone very much at ease because he was able to talk about it."

George Walker not only accepted his own dying, he prepared his own funeral—down to the last detail. He decided what would be sung, what would be said, who would be invited, and even who would sit where. His daughter recalls the day he sent her and her mother down to the church to review the list of hymns with the choir director. The director got so excited over George's choice of music that he said, apparently more than once, "Oh, I can't wait for this funeral!" Finally, Mrs. Walker looked at him with disdain and responded, "Excuse me, but do you realize that you're talking about my husband's death?"

Not only was there intimacy, spirituality, and detailed preparation, there was also humor. "Dad was a great one to laugh with," his daughter said. "They put a shower cap on him as they were taking him up to surgery and I said, 'Dad, you look just like Mrs. Marstead.' Mrs. Marstead was this very large lady who swam at the beach and she'd always go in with a huge bathing cap. That was another of our bonds—much humor, much laughter."

In the final weeks, George drifted in and out of clouds of consciousness. Fever came and went. And his family sat vigil. His daughter gave him sips of water, smoothed his hair, trimmed his fingernails, and rubbed the smooth, soft skin on his back. Then, for hours at a time she simply sat in his presence, in the stillness of that large room, watching the changing season outside the window and writing poetry before a fire, as her father slowly and gracefully left this world.

On the night of November 29, George died. His family closed his eyes, sat with him for a time, and called the undertaker. And then they held the funeral that he, himself, had planned.

Nearly two decades later, on the very same day, November 29, Betty lost her husband. But this time, her experience with death was very different.

Late in October her husband, Ben, mentioned casually that he had lost his appetite. Betty's ears perked up because her husband loved to eat, and so she suggested that they call the doctor in the morning. Some tests were performed, but little was said or done. Over the course of that week, Ben's appetite continued to wane and he had markedly less energy. At Betty's urging, more tests were ordered, other doctors were called in, and finally, in mid-November a doctor called to say that something was "very wrong" with either Ben's kidneys or his liver.

He went into the hospital on November 20 for more tests and wasn't diagnosed with cancer for another four or five days. Betty still remembers vividly the moment they got the diagnosis. "The doctor came in and said, 'Well, we found out what's wrong with you. You've got a real bad booger'—that's what he called it, a horrible name, 'booger'— 'at the bottom of the esophagus. It doesn't look good. We're giving you a little bit of time, but not much.' I was alone with Ben. My face got all red and when the doctor left the room I burst into tears. Ben shrugged his shoulders and said, 'Well, tomorrow will be another diagnosis.' "

Although they both knew, even before they got the diagnosis, that Ben's illness was very serious, they never spoke openly about it; in fact they never even acknowledged aloud how serious the situation was. At one point before entering the hospital Ben had insisted on going to his office to look for his will, and Betty learned later that he had said something to a sister-in-law about being very concerned and afraid. "But Ben and I never spoke about his illness. Ben did say, 'I gather the doctor talked to you.' I said, 'Right.' And then we didn't talk about it."

Chemotherapy was started, not to change the course of the disease, Betty said, but to reduce the amount of fluid Ben's body was producing. His abdomen was constantly swollen even though the doctors drained three or four liters of liquid out of him each day. On the day of the 28th, he was very uncomfortable. The drugs seemed to make him feel sick, Betty said. He had an oxygen tube in his nose and was being given "all kinds of stuff" to relieve constipation. "Everything was either being blocked by the fluid or closing down, and he had this thing harnessed to his nose which he was constantly trying to pull off."

His children and some grandchildren had arrived. He recognized them, but was not up to having any sort of conversation. They got busy making plans to bring him home. But at four o'clock on the morning of the 29th, a son who had stayed the night at Ben's bedside called Betty to say that Ben was sinking and that while there was no hurry, she should come to the hospital. The son and his sister were the only ones there when Ben's breathing stopped. Betty had not yet arrived.

"I was not there," she said tearfully. "I came and Ben had gone, and I had sad feelings about that. I'd like to have been there. He wasn't conscious, but I would have held his hand. I didn't know, didn't know."

Finally, there is the story of John (whose name, for the sake of privacy, has been changed), a young lawyer who died of AIDS early in the epidemic before any very useful therapies were available. From early September until his death in January, John's friends took shifts being with him and, as he grew sicker, caring for him. "All of us would have been happy if he had chosen to die at home," his friend Andy (whose name has been changed as well) said, "but he didn't choose to die at home. John wanted maximum care. Maximum care didn't amount to much in those days, but he had fantasies that there were some people brilliant enough to bring him through it. He wanted everything."

By late December the disease had ravaged his body and he spent most of his time in the hospital—not just any hospital, but a major cancer center devoted to aggressive medical treatment. He was unable to walk and spent much of his time in pain. His body had become skeletal except where it was swollen from edema. His skin was covered with the purple tumors of Kaposi's sarcoma and raw sores from lying in bed. "He was such a horror to look at," Andy said. "If we had not been attending him all along it would have been impossible. He was so monstrous. It was pitiful beyond description."

On New Year's Day, John entered a hospital intensive care unit by his own choosing and was attached to a ventilator and other machinery, which is how he remained until his death ten days later. In the first week, during brief moments of lucidity, he seemed to think he was going to make it, Andy said. "Then I came in one morning and I said, 'You look so peaceful.' He wrote on a slate 'Resigned.' So I hugged him and I kissed him. And after that, I'm not sure he wanted to make it anymore, but he didn't give any instructions to stop the stuff."

His friends had little say about his care in any case, for his parents were now calling the shots. On the last day of John's life, with his respiratory system shut down, his circulatory system barely working, his brain and the rest of his central nervous system only marginally functional, and his mind "resigned," the doctor announced that John's kidneys had failed and asked whether his parents wanted to start dialysis. They said yes.

"I took his mother and father aside and I said, 'This is outrageous. Why are you doing this? You have to let go. You can't keep him here for another three or four days, deteriorating even more. Why would you do that?' " Andy said. "They didn't understand. They had all kinds of guilt. They didn't know what to do."

This is a glimpse of death today. There is no norm, no single picture, not even a handful of categories. Each death is as individual as the person to whom it happens. None is simple. Each is a reflection of the patient, the life he has lived, the people he has loved, the illness he has endured, and the capacity of those around him to accept the reality of death and to do what needs to be done.

ars moriendi

in search of the "good death"

Anyone can see that the best way to go would be something along the lines of George Walker's death. George died relatively late in life, his death was expected and accepted, and he died with minimal pain, in a comfortable place, amidst loved ones. He did not suffer a long period of illness and disability, his dying was not dragged out, and, perhaps best of all, he died at peace with himself and the world.

Our definition of a "good death" can take on all sorts of wonderful details if we look to those fortunate souls, like George Walker, who climb out of their initial denial, anger, and despair to discover that life's final scene is not merely bearable, but in many ways remarkable. Given the chance, people who are terminally ill often develop a profound spirituality, come to terms with their pasts, and forgive others and themselves for any wrongdoing. Some go even further, developing a heightened creativity; they start to write poetry or paint pictures or spin pots. And they find themselves flooded with love and a vivid appreciation of life. After all, there is no longer any pretense that life is limitless, no time for trivial undertakings or superficial relationships. In confronting death, these people embrace life and gain extraordinary strength, clarity, and artistry. They are like the leaves that dangle green all summer long and then suddenly take on brilliant, fiery hues just before they drop from the branches and float gently to the ground.

Dennis Potter, the English writer, talked about this clarity shortly before his own death from pancreatic cancer at age 58. "In a perverse sort of way," he said in a televised interview, "I'm almost serene. I can celebrate life. Things are both more trivial than they ever were and more important than they ever were.

"The 'now-ness' of everything is absolutely wondrous," he said, describing the color, texture, and scent of some lilac blossoms that had bloomed outside his window. "There's no way of telling you. You have to experience it. But the glory of it. The comfort of it. The reassurance. . . . You see the present tense. Boy, do you see it and boy, can you celebrate it."

My own father had much of the same response to life when it grew short. My mother recalls him staring for long moments at the trees and the clouds and even a single blade of grass, holding it up and examining it from different angles, and remarking on how beautiful it all was, how perfect and wonderful every detail of nature and life had become for him. Months before my father died he and my mother took all of us—children, spouses, and grandchildren—to Florida, and I remember that he spent most of that week sitting on a porch just looking at all of us and taking in the sights and sounds and scents.

Absorbing it, drinking it all in. My father had spent most of his life waiting impatiently for something else, hurrying to get somewhere else. But now he was so clearly in the moment, relishing each breath of salty air, the warmth of the sun on his skin, and the rhythmic roar of the waves. More than anything else, he was relishing us, his family, as we sat on the beach before him, digging in the sand with bright plastic shovels, looking through beach bags for sun lotion and magazines, calling out to each other from the water, talking and laughing together. It was rich and vivid and, in the end, intensely "now."

The final days of life can be exceptional for caregivers too because despite the grief, exhaustion, and unimaginable amount of care that is involved, there is often also a deep sense of intimacy and love. Anything trivial or materialistic or selfish disappears, exposing the most stark and touching aspects of life. It is a time of giving and forgiving, of vulnerability and pain, a time when the usual frustrations and annoyances of a day fade and what is truly important becomes clear.

And yet, having said all this, we must be cautious as we try to define a "good death." While most of us would agree that dying like George Walker did, with love and insight and appreciation, is a glorious way to go, a goal we should all strive for, we must be careful not to establish this as our sole criterion. This celebratory dying, this ability not only to come to terms with death but to grow from it, is laudable, but it is not possible in many cases and, believe it or not, is not even desirable in others.

First of all, there is much about death that we can't control. Sometimes it comes so quickly that it is impossible to bring the patient home to die, much less to find any glory in the moment. Sometimes it happens unexpectedly, during a rigorous treatment that held real promise. Sometimes illness is so taxing and debilitating that people do not have the mental capacity, the energy, or the interest in making much of the experience. (Although in many cases what makes it so taxing and debilitating is invasive treatment and the lack of appropriate palliative care.)

Some people can't die at home because of the nature of their illness or because their families cannot or will not, for one reason or another, provide the enormous amount of time and energy that is often required for at-home care. Some patients don't want to be at home because their home life is stressful or because they actually like being in a hospital where they receive constant attention. (One fellow who knew he was dying spent a year in an intensive care unit because he said he didn't mind the tubes and interruptions, and he loved watching television all day and being catered to by the staff.)

Furthermore, some people have no interest in a soul-baring, communal kind of death. Some don't have any interest in talking about death, much less acknowledging it openly, because they have never enjoyed introspection or emotional discussions, or because they simply can't handle the fact that they are dying. Others may choose to die alone because they are ready to go and have no interest in or energy for seeing others or saying good-byes.

Betty Holden, who witnessed the deaths of her husband and her father, loves nothing better than to think about and discuss emotions, feelings, relationships, and spirituality, and if she becomes terminally ill such talks are likely to play a central role in her remaining days, because they always have in her life. But when her husband lay dying, the two of them never spoke about what was happening to him. This wasn't because they were denying it; it was partly because his illness developed so quickly and partly because such conversations simply weren't part of their relationship. That wasn't how they operated. "It would have been an invasion of his privacy to say, 'How do you feel about dying, Ben?' That wasn't his way," Betty said. "Ben never spoke about his feelings. He just wasn't built that way. It's interesting to me that I didn't push more, but I can see why I didn't. . . . I respected Ben's not wanting to talk about it."

The story of an 89-year-old woman who developed leukemia is a good example of just how individual a person's needs are. She decided that she wanted to die without further medical intervention. She had lost her husband many years before and had no surviving family, but with the help of a local hospice, she died according to her own demands and her own needs. She had grown up in a cold, barren land on the edge of Siberia, and was most at home in a cold and barren environment. Her house was large, but she lived in only three rooms: a dining room, a kitchen, and a bedroom. There was no living room, in fact, there was not a couch or a comfortable chair anywhere in the house. There were no curtains, no decorations, no paintings adorning the walls, no fluffy comforters, no soft pillows—just a single crocheted blanket and hundreds of books piled along the walls. She had a small radio, but no television set. The woman spent her final days sitting erect on a wooden chair in her dining room, the only room that was heated. Her bedroom had no heat and in the middle of winter she slept with the windows open. She had one light, hanging over the dining room table, but she didn't turn it on. None of this was done for lack of money or in an effort to save money. It was done because this is how she liked to live. This is how she was most comfortable.

"I'd turn on the light to do my exam and then I'd turn it off and we'd sit in the dark and talk," the hospice nurse told me. "It was cold, very cold. And dark. And it was barren. Her idea of comfort was very different from the standard. But I have to respect what's established. She wouldn't have been comfortable with lights and heat and pillows."

When women tried to reclaim birth they made several mistakes. One of them was assuming that a birth without drugs, surgery, or other intervention, a birth assisted by the father, was *the* good birth, *the* birth that everyone should strive for. Some even insisted that a good birth had to occur at home with a midwife, and others thought the birth should be witnessed by friends and family. But, of course, everyone couldn't have that ideal—some women had complications or risks that didn't allow for such deliveries—and what's more, many women didn't want it. They wanted medications to numb the pain, they wanted all medical precautions in place, they wanted doctors, not midwives, and they wanted or at least didn't mind the surroundings of a hospital. When these women gave birth to wonderful, healthy babies, they were sometimes made to feel as though they had somehow failed; that the birth wasn't "natural." Because the definition of a "good birth" had become so narrow, women who might have gained something from the natural birth movement became alienated from it and even somewhat antagonistic toward it.

We have to be careful how we define our *ars bene moriendi*. We can't establish one single path that is best for everyone, for no one path is right for everyone. And we have to be careful not to romanticize death, creating too rosy or too perfect an image that is impossible to achieve.

We also have to realize that most deaths are neither one extreme or the other, celebratory or intolerable, but rather a mix of many things. Even the very best deaths are communal at some moments and extremely lonely at others. Death may be accepted at some times during the process and denied at others. Or it may be acknowledged, but only in unspoken ways, or only with certain people, or only in reference to certain subjects. A person might speak eagerly about cures while she redrafts a will or hands down her engagement ring or double-checks her life insurance policy. Sometimes death is both expected and accepted, but is also manipulated by medical technology for a variety of reasons—so that the patient can live until a certain important event, for example. Humans have an uncanny ability to believe in many things at once, to embrace opposing views, to plan for the worst while they hope, despite all odds, for the best.

Each of us will approach death in our own way, depending upon the nature of our illnesses, our relationships, our needs and, unfortunately, our resources. Some of us will find new strengths and abilities during our final days; some will discover new patience, appreciation, and intimacy; some will fight to the end, drawing on every type of invasive medical care; some will curl up in bed and post a Do Not Disturb sign on the door; some will be angry and aggressive. Most people will do a little bit of everything, enjoying life at some moments, grieving uncontrollably at others, yelling furiously at times, loving intently at other times, talking about a long future while they wrap up business and say their good-byes. The important thing is that we are somewhat prepared and have the support of our loved ones so that we can have the sort of death that is best for us.

We also have to remember that a "good death" is not just about the obvious and the large. It is not just about the move from the hospital to home, or the withdrawal of aggressive medical treatment. What makes death truly "good" is often reflected in seemingly small and subtle things.

In all the talk about overly aggressive medical care, it is easy to assume that appropriate decisions about medical treatment are all we need in order to achieve a good death for ourselves and our loved ones. If we can just reject certain treatments and escape the excesses of medical technology, we will die well, finding peace and dignity and love at the end of life; if we continue with invasive treatments that hold little promise, we will die poorly. Alas, we have whittled down the extraordinary process of concluding our lives to a single issue: whether or not we are "hooked to machines" in our final days or hours. If only life, or death, were so simple.

Dying well is about much more than saying no to a transfusion or a ventilator. It is about much more than receiving an adequate dose of morphine. Dying well is predicated on who we are and how we love and whether we can find it in ourselves to accept and forgive each other. It is founded not so much on big acts, like "pulling the plug," as much as simple acts—a comment, a look, an embrace, a caress—that help us tie up loose ends and begin the process of letting go. Dying well is not simply about not having what we don't want, but about having what we do want—who we want to see, what we want to say, what might console us, and how we can celebrate the lives that we have lived. But there is no line on the advance directives form where we are asked to explain that we would like to be held or gently stroked, that we would like our grandchildren to be near, that we hope we will be forgiven for any unkindness we have committed, that we want our loved ones to be familiar and easy with us, that we hope they might even laugh and be joyous in our presence even as we near death.

Dying well is about finding peace in the maelstrom, accepting what we can never truly understand, and allowing ourselves to love, wholly and unselfishly, at a time of enormous loss—however that loss occurs. It is about getting our hands dirty and our hearts broken. Dying well begins long before death is imminent, before the brain damage is severe, or the coma irreversible, or the treatment futile, and it requires that we do much more than make decisions about medical treatment.

So, how should we define a "good death"? What should we aim for? We can't draft a detailed description, but we can list a few basic components that, when taken together, make a death "good." Not surprisingly, these factors are not all that different from what makes up a good life: knowledge, respect, love, safety, and comfort.

❧ **In a good death, the patient and family are fully informed and their decisions are respected.** They know what services exist in their community, their rights within the medical system, and the various options available to them. Throughout an illness, they understand the prognosis, they are aware of all the treatment choices available, and they know the goals, benefits, and drawbacks of each. They also understand that any and all treatments can be rejected, that pain and symptoms can be managed, and that people can die at home. If the patient cannot make decisions for himself, his family should have a clear understanding of his wishes, priorities, and fears so that they can, with some sense of unity, make decisions on his behalf.

Once the patient or any surrogate makes a decision about medical care, that decision should be respected by other family and friends, as well as by any health professionals involved in the patient's care.

❧ **In a good death, pain relief and symptom management are not considered an alternative to invasive medical treatment, but an integral and essential part of a continuum of care.** A patient's comfort should be monitored with as much precision and interest as her heart rate and oxygen levels, and any complaints should be addressed immediately and aggressively. (Palliative care experts are trying to get hospitals to include pain as a fifth vital sign, so that it would be monitored regularly along with temperature, blood pressure, pulse, and respiratory rate.) Once comfort is the goal of the treatment, pain should be treated aggressively and medications should not, under any circumstances, be withheld, limited, or delayed.

❖ **Emotional and spiritual pain, which are often overlooked, should receive serious attention.** Physical pain is so intertwined with psychological pain that one cannot be properly treated without the other. This doesn't mean sending in the obligatory social worker or member of the clergy for a quick visit. Fear, loneliness, and existential angst require a far more lasting, intimate, and human touch.

People who face death should have a place where they can speak openly. They should be allowed to express their love, forgiveness, grief, regrets, and fears, but they should also be given room to express their anger and frustrations. They should be reassured that their lives have been, and still are, worthwhile, that they will not be forgotten, and that their loved ones will be okay when they are gone. They should be given the opportunity to review their religious beliefs and talk at length about spiritual issues, which often become vitally important when death looms.

On a more simplistic level, a person who is anxious or afraid may simply need to be held or spoken to gently so that he or she can get through a medical crisis or procedure. We are so quick to respond to pain with medications that we sometimes forget that human compassion and touch are also potent elixirs. A person who is panicked because she cannot take a full breath of air may be helped by a ventilator or tranquilizer, but she might also be calmed by knowing that her daughter is on the way, or because someone speaks softly to her and strokes her hand gently. These approaches won't solve a medical emergency, but they can help. As Dr. Margaret Drickamer, a geriatrician, tells her medical trainees: "Don't just do something; be there.

"In any crisis situation, the first thing you do is sit down," she says. "Take the patient's hand, and if he is short of breath, start stroking his arm at the rate he is breathing and then start slowing down your stroking. It's like the old joke, the first thing you do at a cardiac arrest is take your own pulse.

"Anybody who has felt as though he can't breathe—if you have ever been underwater too long or something like that—knows that that feeling is just horrendous," she says. "People will say, 'Intubate me,' but what they're really saying is, 'For God's sake, do something. I'm totally panicked.' Unfortunately, 'Do something' to most people means shoving a tube down a person's throat. My approach is that you immediately sit down at the bedside and take the patient's hand. You don't run around and panic, because the patient is already panicked enough. I give the patient Ativan, which is a cousin of Valium, and morphine, and I sit down and say, 'You're going to feel better. I'm giving you the medication now.' I'll talk slowly, and often before the medication has even taken effect, the patient is calm again and able to cope."

♣ **Whenever feasible, death should occur in a place where the patient is most comfortable and has the most control over his own life.** In most cases, that means dying at home simply because it is hard to find comfort or control, much less intimacy, in a hospital. Tubes and machines stand in the way, nurses and orderlies walk in without so much as an "excuse me," and roommates prevent any possibility of privacy. Furthermore, once in the system, patients tend to find themselves on a track of aggressive treatment that is difficult to escape.

♣ **The patient and family should be aware that death could come at any time and act accordingly.** No matter where a person is—home, hospital, nursing home—and even if the patient is still pursuing invasive treatment, he and his loved ones should not postpone anything that they want to do or say. If possible, old angers and hurts should be healed or at least put to rest. Whatever love exists should be offered as freely and fully as possible, allowing the person to die in peace and loved ones to grieve without tremendous emotional obstacles in the way.

Beyond these basic ingredients, there is no recipe, no formula for a good death, because one of the most important aspects of a good death is that it is not pinned to anyone else's vision. A good death is not designed by a daughter, a doctor, a friend, a social worker, or a writer; instead, it should suit the unique needs of the person who is ill.

In other words, a good death is one that has been claimed. It is a death in which the doctor or some other health care provider guides the patient and family through the process, without leading them down a particular path. It is a death in which the patient understands the choices before him and can, either directly or through a proxy, choose his own route. It is a death in which the patient's own needs, whatever they may be, are respected.

This is tricky, because loved ones can't help but be a little selfish at a time like this. They don't mean to be. In fact, they want to help the patient more than anything in the world. But they also have their own dire needs and fragile emotions. Someone they love is dying. They have to find a way to cope with this and to find an ending that they can then live with. And so, unwittingly, they pursue the death that suits their own egos, visions, needs, and guilt-ridden consciences. They want to help the patient, but they are using their own personal road map for how death should occur.

For example, daughter Carol may want to stop Mom's therapy and get her home so that Mom can die peacefully and she, Carol, can tend to her every need. Daughter Ann is terrified by the thought of bringing Mom home and thinks that she should stay in the hospital where she will receive whatever treatment is necessary. Son Fred is overwhelmed by guilt because he hasn't called Mom since their dispute two years ago (he didn't even send her a birthday card this year) and he is not ready to let his mother die. He has loads of unfinished business. "What the hell is going on here?" he yells. "Mom would never give up like that. We need to get her over to the specialists at The Major Medical Center." Well, maybe Mom wants more treatment and maybe she doesn't, but no one knows, because they haven't bothered to think about her views and any previously stated wishes. Everyone else is making declarations for her—declarations based on their own needs, not hers.

"Everybody becomes enormously selfish," said Dr. Sherwin Nuland, who has spoken extensively on death since his book *How We Die* was published. "They don't know they're selfish. They all think they're doing what's best for the dying person. But what each member of a family does and what the doctor does is always try to figure out what seems the best from his own point of view."

Family members, loved ones, and the doctor all aim for a death that will give them serenity when they look back on it in the years to come, he explains. "You live your life with a person, you grow up with that person, it's 25, 35, 45 years, and when that person dies, somehow you see their entire lives through the prism, through the lens, of those last months, those last weeks. You can't get that out of your mind. Somehow you know that, and so you want that to be as easy as possible."

Of course it is important that the needs of family members and other loved ones are considered. But what's interesting is that when families look at the medical decisions and care from the perspective of the patient, when they ask themselves "What would *he* want me to do?" rather than "What do I think should be done?", they are apt to be relatively satisfied with the results. They know that they have done the best that they could do.

a note on dignity

Any discussion of a good death cannot come to a close without some mention of dignity, for this is the clarion call, "death with dignity." My own feeling is that the expression has been so overused and its meaning so contorted that we should scrap it. For some people, death with dignity means a "natural" death without invasive medical intervention or machinery. Some say dignity is about remaining lucid or maintaining control over the situation. Others seem to suggest that dignity is reflected by one's outward appearance and bodily function—having your rear end exposed is by definition undignified. Recently the expression has also been used in reference to physician-assisted suicide.

Such views of dignity only return us to those erroneous visions of death as something that should be clean and fluffy and beautiful. The truth is, death is messy. People drool and need their bottoms wiped; they smell and they make unpleasant noises. From a purely physical point of view, they are rarely what one would call dignified. As for the machines, they, by themselves, don't strip a person of dignity. And as for gaining personal control, which has become so critically important in recent years, people retain control in that their wishes are respected and, if at all possible, carried out; beyond that, death is, by its very nature, about letting go of control. When they are dying, people are usually too sick, debilitated, confused, or exhausted to make decisions for themselves; they must relinquish control and trust those around them to pilot their final days for them.

Because we've created this expectation that death should be dignified, without examining what that means, survivors are often left feeling guilty, wondering what they did wrong because their loved one didn't seem particularly dignified at the end. Now people even talk about committing suicide because they are so afraid of losing what they perceive to be their dignity. Is this what we've come to? Creating "dignity" for ourselves administering a lethal dose?

The truth is, dignity has little to do with autonomy or respirators or fecal continence. Dignity is a character trait, like courage or kindness or intelligence. It is something we have within ourselves, not something that is reflected in our physical appearance; nor is it something to which we have a right. It is not something we can demand for ourselves, create for others, or achieve through suicide. And it is not something that we lose simply because we are dying.

Morrie Schwartz, a sociology professor at Brandeis University, is the subject of the best-selling book *Tuesdays with Morrie*, and was interviewed for *Nightline* because he was so philosophical about his dying, and was willing to talk openly about his pain, his reflections on life, and the lessons he was learning in death. In the *Nightline* interview he talked about his mourning and bitterness and bouts of uncontrolled crying. He talked about reviewing his life, letting go of regrets, and repairing broken relationships. He talked about God and his new awareness of "a glowing sense of the connectedness of all of us." He urged others to talk openly about illness without shame, to be compassionate, and to live fully.

Morrie had amyotrophic lateral sclerosis, also known as motor neuron disease or Lou Gehrig's disease. In ALS, the nerves that control muscular activity degenerate, leaving the muscles to atrophy until the person cannot walk or lift a finger. Eventually the muscles that control breathing and swallowing are paralyzed and the person suffocates or chokes to death.

ALS is a horrible, debilitating disease that steals the body, leaving the mind to function within an increasingly useless and burdensome shell. Toward the end of his life, Morrie couldn't feed himself, wipe his bottom, or push his glasses up on his nose when they slipped down. Nevertheless, he had a good death because he got clear answers to all of his questions, considered his choices thoughtfully, and made decisions which were honored. He had a good death because his care was what I would call aggressively holistic; although little could be done about the disease itself, enormous work was put into alleviating his discomfort, making the most of whatever abilities he still had, and providing him with emotional and spiritual support. He had a good death because the people around him respected him and loved him and treated him as a complete and living person, despite the increasingly wretched shape of his body.

Morrie Schwartz also died with dignity, enormous dignity, not because someone gave it to him, but simply because that was part of who he was. He refused to deny his dying or to hide his illness; he refused to be ashamed of his decline or to take blame for it. When asked if losing control of his body was embarrassing, Morrie said, "I have no shame because that's a cultural phenomenon that we've built into us. My dignity comes from my inner self." He hit that nail squarely on the head.

Morrie died with dignity because while his body deteriorated, his soul, his self-respect, and his respect for others remained intact. He developed dignity throughout his life and he maintained it in death. While his emotional openness and deep spirituality may not be for everyone, his willingness to navigate death with courage and honesty is something we can all strive for, and his dignity is something we can all learn from—in death, as well as in life.

II
down a new path

confronting death

addressing our fears and beliefs

So how do we achieve this elusive "good death," or at least improve our odds of achieving it? How do we prepare for our own deaths, and equip ourselves so that we can help our parents, spouses, friends, and others we love when they are terminally ill? How do we move beyond the simple framework of advance directives and learn *ars bene moriendi*?

When I posed this question to Dr. Alan Mermann, chaplain at Yale School of Medicine, who teaches a course on dying to young doctors, he told me a story about a train engineer. The engineer, he said, drove a train from New York to San Francisco on a regular basis. The train tootled through the various cities and towns of the east, but once it got beyond Chicago, it picked up speed, soaring more than 100 miles an hour through vast, empty expanses of land. One day the train was flying rapidly around a long curve when the engineer spotted a freight train derailed across the track ahead. Without hesitating, he grabbed the throttle and pulled it with all his might, propelling the train forward with so much power that it cut right through the blockade. The train suffered little damage and no one aboard was badly hurt. Later, reporters clamored around the engineer, all of them asking the same question: "What made you think to speed up? Why didn't you apply the emergency brake instead?" The engineer explained, "During all the years that I've been an engineer on this train, I've spent hours and hours and hours looking at the rails, going through this town and that town, and thinking of all the possible things that could go wrong and what I might do. When I saw this happening, I'd already thought through the possibilities many times and so I knew exactly what to do."

We all know for a fact that we are headed for a crash. We know that we will die and that we will face the deaths of those we love. We don't know when it will happen or how it will happen or how we will react to it. But like the engineer, we can brace ourselves for the possibilities. We can prepare ourselves, both intellectually and emotionally.

But to do that we need to move beyond the periphery, where we peek with morbid curiosity at the truly horrible and hold intellectual debates about the rights of dying patients, and enter the terrain of death. We need to step closer, and then even closer still, until we feel the cold gust of death upon our souls. This is the frigid inner sanctum, where death is personal and real. It is not an easy place to be, but neither is it as horrible as we imagine.

Before you sign advance directives or make a suicide pact or learn about life support, take a good, hard look at this fellow with the scythe. Explore your own thoughts on death. Think not just about safe, sterile subjects like the medicine and legalities and ethics involved, but about death, the big picture. Death with a capital D. Because when you sign a living will or make a promise to a loved one, you're not talking simply about using a medical procedure or refusing it. You're talking about finality. About mortality. About pain and disease and decline and final good-byes. It is easy to say, "I would never want that procedure," but have you tried to put yourself inside the mind of a dying person? Have you ever really imagined what it is like to make life-and-death decisions for someone whom you can't live without?

In order to handle this ending with any tenderness or finesse, we have to face our fears and begin to accept the reality of death into our lives. For it is our fear, and the resulting denial, that makes us ball up and freeze like a threatened spider when death comes calling. It is our refusal to even imagine the crash that leaves us so stunned when the worst is imminent. We have to accept that the crash will happen. We have to imagine the unimaginable. And we have to confront whatever anxieties and phobias we harbor so that they don't suddenly rear up and block us in the final hour from doing whatever needs to be done.

Some of the more common fears and views of death are outlined here, but you should delve into this subject on your own. Spend some time with it. Roll it around in your mind. Don't obsess; but do explore. You don't have to sit pitifully in the miasma of death, the nauseating fog of dread and pain; but you should examine the reality. Take control of it. What is it, exactly, that makes you panic at two o'clock in the morning about a brain tumor, that makes you put off a visit to a terminally ill friend, that makes your heart race when you contemplate the end of your own life or the life of someone you love? What aspect of death is most frightening for you? What is not frightening? What do you believe about the existence of an afterlife and the meaning of our brief appearance on this planet?

By opening our eyes and exploring our feelings about death, in solitude or with others, we can take hold of our fears, alleviate them, pinpoint the issues that need our attention, become more comfortable with the subject, and prepare ourselves, just a little bit, for what lies ahead. By pulling the Grim Reaper out of the closet, out of the shadows and into the light, and taking a good hard look at him—and doing so over and over again until he is a part of our lives—we can truly begin the process of reclaiming death.

facing fears

I think it was Woody Allen who said, "I'm not afraid of death. I just don't want to be there when it happens." I'm always surprised when people tell me they are not afraid of dying. With the exception of my grandmother, who died a few days shy of her ninety-ninth birthday, had completed all she needed to do in this life, had lost most of her closest friends, and believed absolutely without question in an afterlife, I can't imagine that anyone could have no fear of death, or at least not have a large dose of gut-churning dread. My guess is that most people who say this simply have not given the subject enough thought, for fear of death, as far as I can tell, comes with being human. Ernest Becker, in his Pulitzer Prize–winning book, *The Denial of Death*, argues that we feel not just fear, but terror, and it is our lifelong attempt to deny death that drives almost all that we do.

In any case, if we don't acknowledge our fears, we will be completely stunned when we face the death of a loved one, and we will respond in ways that we will later regret.

What's surprising is that when we do dig into the gloom and grab hold of our true feelings about death, our deep-in-the-soul feelings about it, we often discover that our biggest concerns have nothing to do with medical treatment and prolonged suffering. Oddly enough, the only aspect of dying we have ever discussed or addressed on paper, our medical care, is not even all that critical to us. Our biggest fears, at least when we are standing at a safe distance from death, are often focused on other issues.

Most people have at least some existential angst, for it is nearly impossible to imagine the state of being dead. Even people who believe in an afterlife often have trouble coping with the image of themselves being gone from this world. Where will we be? What happens to the soul, the spirit, the ego, the memories, the relationships, and all those unfulfilled dreams? We have no memory of an existence before this one, but somehow the idea of not existing in some way, shape, or form in the future is unnerving. It's disturbing to imagine the world going on without us—coffee brewing, schoolbuses blocking traffic, our friends getting together, our children and grandchildren growing up. The fun continues but we are erased, blotted out, from each scene.

Coupled with this, most of us have practical concerns. One of the most common fears cited in connection with terminal illness is the fear of being a burden to one's family. We don't want others to have to care for us, to be saddled with enormous bills, or even to worry about us. We also dread death simply because we aren't finished yet; there is work to be done, business to be wrapped up. We have young children to raise or a spouse to care for or a project to finish or a deal to complete or a goal to reach. Maybe we want to contribute something to the world before we go, or we are waiting for our retirement to relax, travel, and spend time with family. We still have journeys to take and dreams to realize.

Then there is the overwhelming sadness that death, or the proximity of death, will bring. Whether we have finished our work or not, we don't want to leave the party. We don't want to miss out on what lies ahead. Like the child who resists bedtime, we want to stay up and see what's going to happen. We want to see how things are going to turn out, who's going to marry whom, how many grandchildren we will have, and whether the space station will work out. We don't want to miss out on any big news or good times or interesting gossip. We want to stay and hang around with our friends and family.

What I find disturbing is that not only will you have to leave the party, but you have no idea when. Which headache, bump, or cough will lead to a deadly diagnosis? Do you have thirty years left, or just a few more days? And how will it happen? Will it be sudden or slow and grueling? The unknown aspect of it all, the surprise attack involved, is unsettling. We control, or seem to control, so much in our lives, but we have no control over the Big Whammy. It's going to come to us and to our loved ones, but we have no idea when or how. It just looms, a flickering possibility, each time there is a new ache or pain. Who wants to do a breast self-exam or get their colon checked under such a shadow? It sometimes seems that if we only knew the timing of our deaths, if we knew how long we get to stay and when we will have to leave, we could face this whole thing a little easier. But then again, maybe not.

I sometimes fear learning that I have a life-threatening disease more than I fear the actual process of dying. I figure that I'll be so sick and drugged in the end I won't know or care about what's happening. But I am terrified at the thought of the diagnosis, the moment when a routine exam or simple biopsy turns out to be not so routine, when the doctor turns to me and says, "I've got bad news." I fear those early days when I am deciding about brutal treatments and dealing with family members and trying to digest the whole horrible nightmare.

I had a new, but fortunately very brief, thought on all this after attending a relative's funeral not long ago. Family members and friends were standing around, drinks in hand, reminiscing. They remembered the best in this person, but mostly they rolled their eyes as they recalled some of her less favorable traits. All I could think was, "What will they say about me?" Suddenly, at that moment, the saddest thing about dying was the thought that people's memories of me might be mediocre, or worse. I want to go out with a little glory. The service should be packed, with one tribute following the next. "What a terrific person she was," I want people to say. But instead I picture a gathering of my immediate family. "She was okay," they say. "A little pushy, but okay." How depressing.

A more disconcerting thought than that of actually being dead, for most of us anyway, is imagining the process of dying. While the physical decline and pain may be less of an issue for a young, healthy person who feels invincible, it can become an overriding concern once someone has been sick and has experienced the onslaught of both illness and treatments. It's horrible to imagine harsh treatments, unremitting pain, full-body nausea and fatigue, not to mention the dependency brought on by serious illness. Then there is the loss of usefulness, loss of looks, loss of control, loss of respect. Some people have very specific fears about the process—they don't want to be on dialysis like their sister was, or they don't want to ever lose a limb, or they can't stand the idea of going bald.

Personally, I don't like the idea of people treating me differently. I wouldn't want them whispering their sympathies or looking sadly at me. I wouldn't want them being nice in a false sort of way, or avoiding me because I was sick. I don't like the idea of them saying, "Did you hear . . . ?" to each other. I wouldn't want them watching my every act and deciding whether I'm being stoic or wimpy. Some people keep news of a serious illness a secret from even their dear friends, in part because they don't want to endure such sympathy or scrutiny.

A fear of loneliness is sometimes mixed into this brew, for surely dying can be lonely, especially in this day and age when people dodge anything hinting at serious illness or death. Even if others are compassionate, they can't share your pain with you or begin to understand what you're going through. Ten months before she died, Barbara Rosenblum wrote in her book, *Cancer in Two Voices*, "If you think standing by yourself waiting for someone to talk to you is lonely, if you think holidays alone are lonely, if you think that not having a relationship for a long time is lonely, if you think that the long, frightening nights after a divorce are lonely—you cannot know the aloneness of one who faces death, looking it squarely in the eye."

Mixed in with these relatively rational fears are the less rational ones, the bizarre ones that sneak into our logical minds and refuse to leave. These are the ones we hesitate to admit. Some people can't stand the thought of their bodies being mutilated or cremated, or decaying in the ground. Some have visions *à la* Edgar Allan Poe of being buried alive and then clawing at the top of a coffin as the air is slowly used up. One person I interviewed told me that when he thinks about death he can't help but imagine himself cold and lonely in a coffin. These fears seem ridiculous when spoken, when they are brought to light; nevertheless, these are the shadowy fears that hide under our beds.

Sometimes what really haunts us is not the thought of leaving the party ourselves, but of seeing someone we love leave. We don't want to be left on this earth without this person. We are unable to contemplate death or even discuss it because we are so terrified of being beaten to the grave by someone we need. "Please God, just let me go first," we pray.

Most of us don't fear any one thing; we harbor a mixed bag of fears. And at times, mingled with the dread and worries, there is also a vague and odd sense of relief, for death means that we won't have to hurry or try or hurt anymore. We won't have to fail or worry or struggle. We know the fight will be over and we can rest.

Whatever your own fears and dreads and concerns are, tease them out, one by one, examine them carefully, try to address them, and then revisit them at another time, for they will change. The less logical fears should deflate under serious scrutiny. As for concerns about the ego and the disappearance of the Self, well, that requires deep soul-searching and a lifetime of religious and spiritual review. Do we continue to exist, and what does life mean in its finite form? These are questions that have kept theologians engaged for thousands of years.

Are you worried about leaving things unfinished, unfulfilled, unresolved? Then find time to take a postponed trip, to mend a frayed relationship, to finish a half-baked project. Are you frightened by the legacy you will leave? Think about the memories you can still create, the impact you can still have, the gifts you can still give. What might you bestow on others? How might you become the kind of person you want them to remember? Are you afraid of pain? Talk with your doctor and loved ones about this issue so they know that you want them to treat pain aggressively. You might also learn some techniques, such as meditation and biofeedback, for easing pain.

None of this is easy. And examining your fears won't make them disappear. Fear and dread will always be there. But it is better to address them than to ignore them and then discover later that they are there, like some horrible warts clinging to your soul, boulders blocking your path.

seeing the reality

Perhaps the most important thing you can do is actually imagine death. Next time its ghostly image creeps into your thoughts, fight the urge to cast it out, to switch channels. Instead, invite it in. Walk through your own death and the deaths of those you most love—not in one sitting, but over time. Imagine yourself getting bad news and moving through the process. Imagine standing at the bedside of your parent, partner, sibling, child. Imagine yourself facing death in one way or another. Of course, most of this is wholly unimaginable, but trying to do so is a good exercise. Like the engineer who envisioned the crash, it prepares us.

I have done this many times now. I imagine how I might respond if I were told that I had a terminal illness. I think about how I would react if I were caring for my husband, refusing further treatment for my mother, saying good-bye to a friend. I think how I might feel, whether I could act, and what I might regret. I walk through the process, and as I do so, I sob pitifully into my pillow. Then I lie still, exhausted but not sleepy, staring out the skylight above my bed at the darkness beyond. I roll onto my side and see the bright red numbers on my clock. Then I creep quietly down the hallway, going first into one room and then another, so that I can gaze upon my sleeping children. I stroke their soft hair, listen to their gentle breathing, pull up the covers, kiss their sweet cheeks, and draw in their sweet scents. Then I go back to bed, oddly fulfilled. Cold from the trek, I snuggle close to my husband, feel his warmth, love him enormously, and fall asleep.

Imagining the dreaded dragon is not simply an exercise in tears; it prepares us. It forces us to imagine the unimaginable—what would we do, how would we act—and it starts us on an interesting grieving process that is sad but also wonderful. Wonderful because we wake up in the morning and can seek out the beloved person we've imagined losing, spend time together, hug, laugh, and play. Hallelujah. We still have time together.

My mother is vitally important to me. She is in her seventies, and while still active and youthful, she has chronic lung disease. One bad cold or too much exertion could put her over the edge. With rest and therapy—inhalers, antibiotics, regular sessions with the respiratory specialist, daily back-pounding to loosen the mucus, and so on—she might be able to keep this thing somewhat at bay. But she is not the best patient, and her condition seems to get progressively worse. As her coughing becomes harder and more constant, her breathing more strained, and her body more frail, I am tempted to confine her to her room, enforce daily therapy sessions, and monitor her every move with a masterful glare and an unwavering voice. *I will stop this process from happening. You will not move from this spot if that is what it takes to keep you alive. You can't die. Not ever. I won't let you. Get in bed and take your antibiotics.*

As I have thought about all of this, I have gleaned this bit of truth: one day I will have to let her go. No matter what I do, no matter how many antibiotics she takes, my mother is going to die someday. She is not likely to live to be 99, as her mother did. This is a horribly large and chalky pill for me to swallow, and each time I try it gets caught in my throat, leaving me unable to breathe. My mother is my lifeline. A sweet angel who has made my life okay at its very least okay times.

Confronting this has changed the shape of our relationship, and of my own life. It has allowed me, as I say, to grieve while I still have her. I can call her. I can go see her. I can watch as she gets down on her knees and plays with my children until they are shrieking in delight. I can lie in the grass with her and stare at the treetops, while we share our strangest thoughts, most embarrassing memories, and rampant insecurities. Best of all, I can hug her. With her arms wrapped around me, I am like a spent battery being recharged, and I know that she is too. I will miss her, more deeply than I can possibly imagine; but I love that I still have her.

This grief—what experts would call "anticipatory grief"—has prepared me, a little bit, for what lies ahead. I think that I will make reasonable decisions about her medical care if I am ever in such a position. I don't believe I will push it beyond what she would want. I know how to comfort her. And I am pretty sure I will be able to say good-bye, for we are well aware that the time will come one day, and so there is nothing unsaid, nothing unshared, nothing unknown.

It's been a desperately sad process, but I am, I believe, far more prepared for what lies ahead because of it. I appreciate my mother more than ever before. And I am also learning to let go, to let her live life her own way, which means fully and unhampered. Oh, I still wag my finger at her, give her my sternest look, and suggest she skip the next tennis game or swim in the ocean, but then I watch her go and I am glad that she is so enjoying her life, even if she might be cutting it a tad short. I realize, at those moments, that my urge to protect her is largely selfish, that I want her to stay well for me. I have to release her from my clutches, just as she let me go, allowed me to waltz out into this crazy world, so many years ago.

contemplating our beliefs

Sometimes I get a shade embarrassed when someone turns my way and innocently asks what my latest book is about. I usually pause for a moment, wishing the conversation hadn't taken this turn, and then I say it: "Death." The questioner and any others who happen to be listening are silent for a beat and then they let out a little "Oh" and say something like, "Well that's awfully cheery of you." It sometimes feels as if I have opened a window and let in a blast of icy cold night air, or drawn a large, haunting shadow over a lovely evening. I have silenced the players. Caught them off guard.

At this point the conversation usually veers quickly onto another track, but once in a great while one person—typically someone who has lost a loved one—says with genuine interest, "Really?" and then he starts talking about something he experienced or thought about or read about. Reluctantly, one or two others join in and then, if the mix of people is good, the conversation picks up speed and soon everyone is enrapt in a discussion about, believe it or not, death.

The fact is that while most people are not immediately open to talking about death and virtually everyone is taken aback when the subject is first raised, pretty much everybody has something to say about it. Everyone has thought about death, even if they have never thought about it in depth or discussed their thoughts with others.

One issue that arises in these discussions is, is there an afterlife? Is my dear departed mother still around, still present, in some form or another? Is she content, happy, or troubled? Can she communicate with me? Will *I* continue in some other life? Will I see others whom I have lost? People tend to have strong beliefs about an afterlife, even though they may or may not have spent a lot of time thinking about it. Most have a gut reaction, a firm stand based on fervent emotion, religious study, childhood lessons, or a memorable story: Moments after so-and-so died a beautiful butterfly hung around my back door; just before he died he spoke of a light or a person beckoning; I often hear her voice and sense her presence.

There are no right answers, of course. The idea of an afterlife has no scientific basis; it can neither be proven nor disproven. But the questions are important. They help us to shape and clarify our views about life, death, and dying. They help us prepare for death and give death context in our lives. They help us to begin the process of speaking more openly and honestly about death and preparing for it.

What do you believe? Not what do you want to believe or what do you think you are supposed to believe, but what do you truly, in your most honest moments with yourself, believe? Is there an afterlife? If so, what is it like? Who will you see there? Will you be able to check on those who are still alive? Do those who have died speak to you now? How might your behavior in this life shape your death or any existence that might follow? How does the existence or absence of an afterlife color your view of death?

Religions around the world are largely based on finding some meaning for death in our lives and understanding what happens after death. Most religions view death not as an ending but as a beginning or a transition. Life as we know it, here in our earthly bodies, worried about what's for lunch and whether we will find a good parking space, is merely part of a greater journey. When we die, we don't stop being; we pass on to the next stage.

Religious beliefs, when they are strong and an integral part of one's life, provide a framework for death, a way to include it in one's life, to prepare for it, and then to approach it. This structure and continued preparation, more than the actual details of the particular belief, help to make mortality and the process of dying more manage-

able. Sylvia Vatuk, an anthropology professor at the University of Illi-
nois in Chicago who has studied India and the Hindu culture extensively, says that elderly Hindus discuss death openly and comment
frequently on how they have lived good, long lives and are ready for
death. "Doubtless they talk this way not only because it is considered
culturally appropriate to cultivate equanimity in the prospect of
death," she says, "but because the very act of repeatedly speaking of
it helps them to achieve that state."

Every now and then I envy my grandmother, who didn't believe
there was an afterlife; she knew it for a fact. At 98, she wasn't worried
about leaving the party; she was anxious about missing it. For the
party was not here, but on the other side. Her husband and dearest
friends had all passed away and as far as she was concerned they
were at a giant cocktail party in the sky and she was the only invitee
who still hadn't shown. The problem was, her driver was nowhere in
sight. She was as healthy as an ox (she rode a stationary bike three
miles several times a week) and sharp as a tack (she sent birthday
cards, on time, to 15 grandchildren, and could still remember the
rules of the games she had played as a child).

Every year, late in the fall, Grandma would settle down in front of
her television set to watch the Army-Navy football game, not because
she was a sports fan, but because she and her husband, a Navy man,
had watched this particular game together when he was alive, and she
was quite sure that he was somehow still watching it. This was as
close as she could get to him, given their situation. It was her little
romantic rendezvous.

One day Grandma got sick and several days later, ready and willing, she died. Here's the kicker: she took her last breath hours
before the start of the Army-Navy game. There was no doubt about

her timing. Finally, Grandma was going to watch the Big Game with her man.

For people like me, who don't have my grandmother's unwavering faith, a question arises: if there isn't some sort of afterlife or continued existence, then what happens to us when we die? Do we simply turn into good compost? And if that's the case, then what's the point of life? Why are we here? What do we want to accomplish in our brief stint upon the stage and what difference does it make?

talking about dying

conversations bring
understanding and intimacy

One of my aunts, Jane Morton, says that the subject of death has always been off-limits for her. "I was brought up to believe there were certain things you didn't talk about," she said. "And death you did not talk about. Ever."

So she never discussed death or anything related to death with her father or her mother. Now both her parents are gone and she deeply regrets her unwillingness to discuss death, to contemplate death, or to be near death. She regrets that she didn't know her parents' beliefs and fears and needs, that she was not able to explore this terrain with them.

Despite all her regrets, she still finds it almost impossible to mention the "D" word. The taboo against such talk is so strong in her, the lesson that it is impolite and upsetting is so ingrained, that at 78, she has never discussed death with her husband or her children, even though, she says, she desperately wants to.

"I'm eager to talk about it. I want it all in black and white—the finances, the burial, religious issues, what each person really truly wants, all of it," she said. "But it's not a natural thing for me to bring up this subject."

Jane's sentiments are not remarkable. Most of us don't go beyond simple, vague promises and offhand comments. Like Jane, we sense that this subject is offensive, awkward, depressing.

The British sociologist Geoffrey Gorer said in his writings on death that today the subject of death has become as unmentionable as sex was during Victorian times. Dr. Elisabeth Kübler-Ross calls death "the last and greatest taboo." This was not always the case, of course, nor is it the case today in many cultures and religions. At one time, Ariès explains in his volume on death, people "were afraid to die; they felt sad about it, and they said so calmly. But . . . their anxiety never crossed the threshold into the unspeakable, the inexpressible. It was translated into soothing words and channeled into familiar rites. People paid attention to death. Death was a serious matter, not to be taken lightly, a dramatic moment in life, grave and formidable, but not so formidable that they were tempted to push it out of sight, run away from it, act as if it did not exist, or falsify its appearances."

Talking about death—at length and repeatedly—is crucial if we are to change the way we die. First of all, we have to know how our loved ones feel, and share our own fears and beliefs and hopes with them. Otherwise, we will enter this alien terrain, this forbidden realm, at a time of consuming loss and pain, and we'll be forced to guess our loved ones' wishes or have them guess ours.

Maybe your loved ones would make pretty good guesses. Maybe they know you so well that no detailed discussion is necessary. But research shows that most people appointed as health care proxies have no more idea of what a person would want in a specific situation than they would if they had been chosen randomly from the general population. Even if you trust your proxy to make the right decisions for you, those decisions will be far easier for him to act on if he has talked with you about it and has heard your views.

Second, if you have talked about death when all involved are relatively healthy, the subject won't be quite so off-limits when you really need it, when you or your loved ones are ill and decisions need to be made, or at least discussed. If you have touched on the subject already, it will be that much easier to ask tough questions, get information, and start making decisions when death looms.

Finally, go beyond your health care proxy and talk with your doctor about all this (and have your parents, spouse, and other loved ones talk to their doctors). The doctor needs to know your views, and you need to know whether the doctor understands and respects those views.

broaching the subject

How do you begin such a conversation with a loved one, and how do you then push it beyond vague statements about "pulling the plug"? How do you get your spouse to respond seriously to your concerns? How do you assure your elderly father that he shouldn't take your questions the wrong way? How do you even mention the word "death" to some-one you love? *Mom, what are your thoughts on dying?* It just doesn't slide neatly into a conversation.

To discuss how you might like your own dying to be handled, choose a trusted person to be your health care proxy and then talk to this person about your views.

As for getting someone to talk about their views, or even getting them to think about death, that is a little more difficult. Remember, it is far easier to have this conversation when death is not yet an issue, so it's better to move on this sooner rather than later. (If it is already "later," go ahead and broach the subject as gently as possible. You might use a recent setback as an opening, asking if a recurrence were to be more serious, what would the person want in terms of their treatment, and what would they find comforting.)

The proxy route works equally well when the tables are turned. Explain to your loved one that she should have advance directives—that you have them yourself—and that in addition to the paperwork, she needs to talk in depth with her proxy about her specific wishes and thoughts.

Another way to bring up the subject, either to discuss your own views or to get someone else to explain his or hers to you, is to discuss the illness or death of a friend or acquaintance and how you might have done things the same or differently. Or you might raise the subject in regard to an article you have read, or this or some other book, or some related news item you heard.

If nothing works, ask some other friend or relation, or maybe the person's doctor or lawyer or clergyman, to start the conversation. Your parent or spouse, or whoever, might be uncomfortable talking about death with you for some reason, and might be more willing to open up to another person.

*   *   *

However you initiate the first conversation, do it at a time and in a place where you won't be interrupted, hurried, or distracted. Stress that this conversation is deeply important to you, so the other person doesn't take it too lightly.

When someone else is sharing their thoughts with you, really listen to what they say. Open yourself up to their views. It's easy to paint someone else's views with your own colors, to assume that you know what someone else thinks, or that you know what is best, and then fail to hear what is being said. Also, be careful that you don't accidentally dismiss any comments, respond judgmentally, or let the conversation be cut off by broad statements or jokes. Joking is not necessarily bad; it can ease some of the discomfort, but it can also derail the process. Whatever is said, try to push further, dig deeper, so that you fully understand the other person's views. "Why do you say that? Why would you not want that? What if I didn't think that was the way to go?"

Once you have spoken your mind, ask the other person to explain his understanding of what you have said, so you are sure he has it right. Later, write down some of the key points and store your notes along with any other advance directives. Also, return to the subject regularly, always reviewing, updating, and reiterating what's been said before.

Conversations about death may be awkward and not terribly informative at first, but don't feel defeated. As you become more familiar with the topic, the discussions should become easier and more enlightening. You might stumble some. You might cry some. You might need a few hugs. This is sorrowful stuff. But the tears aren't bad, and with time, these discussions might take you to new and unexpected places, promising for all involved a better dying, but also leading you to a deeper level of intimacy with those you love.

what to discuss

Death is a big subject that can take you in all sorts of directions. A number of topics are raised throughout this book, particularly in the pages that follow. But these are only starting points. Don't let them limit you in any way. Build on what interests you, skip topics, add new questions, or explore the suggested questions further. As you think of new questions or concerns, call your loved ones and discuss them while they are fresh in your mind. Don't rein yourself in.

Whatever you do, do not simply run through a quick list of instructions—"When I'm dying, skip the ventilator, any artificial feeding and all the rest; just let me go quickly." This doesn't give your proxy any particularly useful information.

Talking about death means talking about life. It means getting to know each other on a whole new level. It means understanding what someone finds frightening, painful, or comforting. And it means preparing each other for that moment when it is time to say good-bye, to let go, and to take some responsibility for how death occurs. Talking about death is an adventure into someone else's thoughts, as well as into your own soul. It forces you, yet again, to imagine death and prepare for it. Could you really let your parent or spouse go? Could you say no to a treatment that might delay death? Could you say good-bye?

Talk about the illness and death of someone you know. If you haven't witnessed a death, talk to people who have—as many people as you can. Also review the stories about death in this book. What was good about a particular death? What was bad about it? What might have been done differently? What would you want your loved ones to do in a similar situation? If the death was not good, how did it get off track and how might that have been avoided? Was the person comfortable? Could he or she have been made more comfortable? Were loved ones supportive or distant? Did the health care system work? Were the doctors helpful? Talk about your reactions to these stories. What upset you? What moved you? Why?

Talk about your fears of death and your spiritual beliefs. Discuss the various treatment options and possibilities for care outlined in the chapters "Choices in the End" and "The Possibilities." Talk about the issues someone should consider when making decisions about treatment, and which ones would be most relevant. How much would you want to know or be involved in any decisions, assuming you were cognizant? Do you want your family to err on the side of going too far with treatments or stopping them too soon? What would you imagine to be comforting at such a time? Does the idea of meditation or religious counsel sound calming to you, or does it make you squirm? Would you rather someone turn on some favorite music or a funny video? How do you feel about alternative therapies or new-age rituals? What might worry you at such a time? Where would you want to be? Who would you want to see? Is there any relationship you need to patch up or secrets you want to divulge before you die? Also, review the practical matters listed later in this chapter. Is there any unfinished business you need to attend to? Do you have burial and funeral instructions? How do you feel about organ donation? The possibilities are endless.

Remember, talking about death is an ongoing process. It will take many conversations before you fully understand your loved one's views and preferences—or your own. And once you have a handle on them, they are bound to change. A young person is likely to feel different than an older person, and a person who has never experienced the side effects of chemotherapy or the loneliness of the ICU or the sensation of Death's breath upon her face is likely to approach the subject from a different perspective than someone who has.

conversations with mom

My mother always said that she wants to be "unplugged" when she's "at that point," and she has even said that she would like to be "done in" if she is ever "like that." But the two of us never ventured much beyond these comments. I am her designated health care proxy and for some time I assumed that I knew what I needed to know. Mom didn't want to be left in a hospital room, hooked to machines, when there was nothing left of her mind and no real expectation that she would get better. No problem.

But then I started writing this book and I realized that I had to clarify things. The truth is that while I could say no to life support for my mother under certain conditions, I am not sure whether I could go so far as to lace her applesauce with arsenic.

So the two of us talked, and talked, and talked, and we discovered a number of things along the way. First of all, I realized that my mom, like many people, is not afraid of respirators and feeding tubes as much as she is afraid of being a burden. She does not want her children, or anyone else for that matter, to have to care for her. She does not want to be an emotional, physical, or financial drain. She does not want us to jeopardize our careers or family life in order to care for her. That was what she was thinking about when she said, "Do me in."

I asked her about Dad's death. Did she view that as a burden? Did she see his care as a drain? Would it have been easier if he had taken a vial of pills, which he had actually stored away for just such an occasion? No, she said, of course not. We talked about what caring for him had meant to us, what was hard about it and what was rewarding, and if there were any aspects of it we wished we hadn't had to do, which there weren't. We agreed that his care had not been a chore for us, but an honor and a privilege, a gift that has stayed with us.

Wouldn't all of this be the same if she were dying? Wouldn't she want us to have that same sort of time together, time when we, her children, could care for her and love her and say our final good-byes? Wouldn't that process help us deal with this tremendous loss? Well, she said, she guessed so.

As we talked further, it became clear that her major concern was avoiding long-term care. Taking care of her for a month or two was one thing. But what if she needed care for an extended period? That, she said, would be horrible. She didn't want to be hunched over in a wheelchair, shaking or drooling or staring at the television, with nary a clear thought for years on end. But again, she was less afraid of her own pain or disability than she was worried that her care would be cumbersome for others.

I had to think long and hard about this because I have met the sons and daughters of frail, elderly people. I have interviewed them and written about them. I know about constant care—the cost, the guilt, the anger, and the stress it entails. I know that in these cases, quite often, death is the only relief. But I have also seen these same sons and daughters hugging their parents tenderly, fussing over their hair and clothes, making sure they eat, and adjusting their pillows. I have seen them look at their parents with such enormous love and devotion that it breaks my heart. As exhausting as it all was, many of them tell me later, they would do it again. Could I kill my mother, or even refuse her a round of antibiotics, just because taking care of her was hard work?

I told her that I could say no to aggressive medical treatments if her life seemed to have no joy, no value, if she were struggling through each day and treatment held little promise. I could even say no to less aggressive treatments, a round of antibiotics or a transfusion, if she was suffering and, again, the treatment held little chance of changing her circumstances. (But I offered no promises. Never make promises, for you simply don't know what lies ahead.) I also told her that if her care became more than her children could manage, we would move her into a nursing home or hire plenty of help, which luckily we can afford to do.

But I also told my mother that caring for her was something her children would want to do, that we might even fight over the privilege of doing it. I explained that letting people care for you is okay. In fact, it can be a gift in itself, for we, her children, had much we wanted to give, and she should allow us to do that. If she refused to let us care for her simply because she didn't want to be a burden, she would cheat us out of a rich and healing experience.

We have talked many times about all of this and each time new issues are raised. Each conversation has given me more insight into what she wants at the end, and what I will need to do for her. Each of those conversations has brought us closer, opening us up to the extraordinary hurt that lies ahead, revealing how very deeply we love each other, and reminding us of what we still have, right now, today.

Two conversations in particular stand out in my mind. One occurred after I had been told, by several hospital and hospice nurses, that people often die when their loved ones are out of the room. Family members and friends are at the bedside around the clock and then, during that one moment that they are all gone, the person up and dies. Loved ones feel cheated because they weren't there, and they feel sad that this person was alone at the moment of death. (I have been told that this happens because patients do not want their loved ones to see them go. They want to spare them that pain. Personally, I think it is also because having visitors is so stimulating that people hang on, just as one resists sleep when there is company in the house. When the gathering dissipates and the room falls silent, they are able to give in to death.)

Thinking about this, I called my mother and I told her that when she is close to death, she should feel completely comfortable dying in my arms. She doesn't have to die like this, but I don't want her to ever feel that she should protect me from it. The truth is, I would very much like to be with her, holding her, stroking her, kissing her, at such a time. Mom responded that she has a vivid image of me putting my daughter to sleep when she was a baby. I would hold her in my arms, smooth back her fine blond hair, stroke the soft skin along the edge of her face, and then run my finger down the bridge of her nose, as her eyes began to close. That, my mother told me, is what she wants me to do when she is dying. That, she said, seemed to be a wonderful way to go.

The other conversation came up after a dear friend of ours told me that she worried that her death would deeply hurt her children. She had been devastated by her father's death, and she was concerned about leaving her children with the same overwhelming grief. Even though her children are grown with children of their own, she knew that they would be irreconcilably wounded by her death. She said that my mother held the same fear about me.

I thought about that for some time and then, as part of our continuing conversation, called my mother in a torrent of emotional overload, and said something incomprehensible about how she mustn't worry about me when she's dying. (I don't know how my mom puts up with me.) I told her that her death would change my life. I couldn't lie about that. I would be devastated, but I would also be okay. I had my own family now and my dear siblings, and I would be okay. Sad, really, really sad, but okay. But, I blubbered on, "I have to know that I can cry without upsetting you, and I want you to know that you can cry too, because we will need to be able to cry together. I couldn't stand it if we buried all our aches and tried to protect each other just when we need each other most. Do you know what I mean?" Even though I didn't make any sense at all, Mom knew exactly what I meant, because she always does.

We agreed that we could cry and hold each other when she was dying, the mere thought of which got us crying and saying how much we loved each other, but it also got us laughing over the fact that we were being so mushy in the middle of a sunny afternoon.

This is how these conversations sometimes go.

practical details

My neighbor and dear friend Lou Ann Walker is a great worrier and a great planner. Coming from a line of funeral home directors, she has given the issue of death a good deal of thought. "I think about it *a lot*," she says. What she thinks about is this: Losing her husband, who is much older than she; what will happen if she dies first and her husband is left to raise their young daughter; and her fears of a prolonged and agonizing death. The latter she has seen all too clearly. She tells of a quadriplegic aunt who was on the brink of death for 25 years, and a diabetic uncle who was always at risk of going into a coma. She knows full well that sickness and death can go on for ages and she doesn't want such a thing for herself. She adds quickly that she also does not want anyone performing an autopsy on her, that she does not want to donate her organs, and that she does not, under any circumstances, want to be cremated. "Put it in the ground and leave it alone," she says with a characteristic shrill of disgust. "I do *not* want my body ripped and tossed around. There's a certain sanctity that I want preserved."

However, Lou Ann has never talked to her husband about where she will be buried, and the two of them have not determined how they will handle each other's bodies after death, despite her strong feelings on the subject. "He'll say, 'Just cremate me. Throw me around,' and I'll get so upset that the conversation ends. I don't want to hear that. I cannot deal with it. That image of a body going up in smoke, uh-uh. No way. So we don't talk about it."

"But if that's what he wants. . . ." I start to ask.

"Then I will force myself to do it, but it's horrendous to think about it," she answers. If her husband favors cremation, isn't there a chance that's what he will do with her body, I ask. Her face freezes. "Oh," she says with a pause. "I never thought of that. I'd better talk to him right away." Then she adds with a grin, "For someone who thinks about death a lot, I really don't think about the particulars very much, do I?"

One way to figure out what you need to talk about is to imagine the situation and then list your concerns and address each one. If you got hit by a car tomorrow, what would your survivors need to know? What if your spouse or parent died? What would you need to know? Do you know where your husband keeps the key to the post office box? Did your mother ever tell you who was to inherit her engagement ring? Do you have access to your parents' will? The practical questions are endless, and obviously there are some things survivors will have to figure out on their own, but here are some examples of the issues you might discuss—or at least cover in a letter of instruction that is kept with your will:

🌿 **Who needs to know?** Who should be contacted when you die? Is there a list of dear friends and their phone numbers, people who would want to be told? What about business partners, employers, lawyers, doctors, accountants, insurance companies, pension contacts, and the like?

🌿 **Who gets what?** How is your personal property to be handled? Although your will might give general instructions, what about personal items, like a diary, a wedding ring, medals, letters, books?

🌿 **Business matters.** How would someone go about clearing up your business dealings, collecting outstanding bills, and finding necessary paperwork, such as a business ledger, receipts, contracts, rental agreements, titles, or deeds? What should they do with your office supplies or research materials or a half-finished manuscript?

🌿 **Personal finances.** Does someone know where you keep important papers, such as your will, insurance policies, checkbook, credit or debit cards, tax returns, retirement plans, investment and bank statements, titles and deeds to personal property, hidden valuables, and the key to the safe-deposit box? If you keep important information on your computer, do survivors need a password in order to access it?

🌿 **Young children.** If both parents die, who will raise any young children? Has a guardian been named in a will and have you talked to that person about their job and your children's needs? How will they support the children? Has a trust been established? Is there some way your children can learn about you when they are older? (You might want to write letters to your children discussing your beliefs and values and feelings about their upbringing. Or you might leave instructions that should you die, your friends are to write letters about who you are, special moments they remember, and what was important to you. You might also be sure that you are in some of the family videos so young children can see your face and hear your voice when they are older.)

Are *you* the person in someone else's will designated to care for their children? What do you need to know in order to care for those children?

❧ Odd details. Does someone know how to take care of a second home, a special pet, or your rare plants? Do you have diaries or letters that you don't want others to see?

❧ Funeral and burial arrangements. What are your thoughts regarding a funeral or memorial service? Are there songs, poems, or book passages that you would like included, or specific clergy that should preside? Where do you want to be buried? Do you want to be cremated, and, if so, what should be done with your ashes? Do you want any special marker or planting? What should be included in an obituary and where should it be sent? (Prepaying for a funeral, which has become popular lately, is not necessarily a good idea, as this may not allow for a change in plans and can cost more than you are led to believe. It's better to set up a special account to cover funeral costs if you are worried about them.)

While it is helpful to explain your preferences and make suggestions, especially if you feel strongly about something, keep in mind that these rituals are for the survivors. Planning a burial and funeral—picking out the music and flowers, and deciding what will be said and by whom—is all part of the grieving process. So don't go overboard doing it all yourself. Leave some room for survivors to find their own ways of memorializing you.

☙ **Organ donation.** When survivors are asked about organ donation, they are usually taken aback. It's something they haven't thought about and, at such a time, something they can't imagine. Or, no one is even asked about organ donation, even though the deceased had expressed wishes to be an organ donor.

Healthy hearts, lungs, kidneys, corneas, skin, and other organs and tissues are desperately needed. Donating organs does not mean that a body is disfigured; in fact, in most cases you can still have an open casket. If you are interested, sign the organ donor portion of your driver's license and, most important, make sure your family knows about and understands your wishes. (For more information, go to www.organdonor.gov on the Internet, or call the United Network of Organ Sharing at 800-355-7427.)

choices in the end

a look at medical issues and options

We talk about not being hooked to machines at the end, but what does that mean? What exactly is life support? What does it do? What does it look like? What is so horrible about it? What do we give up if we refuse it? And while we are on the subject, what are DNR, artificial nutrition, and brain death? As we talk with our loved ones, what is it, really, that we are talking about?

This chapter looks at the practical side of death: what sorts of tests, medications, machines, and other treatments frequently come into play at the end of life, and how medical decisions are made at such a time. What is important, however, is not your grasp of technical minutia, but your understanding of the general issues involved.

Armed with such information, you will be able to talk about death in real terms rather than in vague wishes, and you will be better equipped to ask questions and make informed decisions in the face of death.

We are not helpless; there is much we can do to regain control over our own dying or the death of our loved ones. But keep in mind, there is no assurance that you will do it in the way that you might have imagined or planned. There will always be things that are out of our control, and things that we didn't expect. Each death requires different responses and actions from loved ones. We won't handle any of them perfectly. We will say the wrong things and miss opportunities and make decisions that we later question or regret. There is no avoiding that.

In fact, one of the things we need to do is to accept the fact that despite all of our efforts, we or our loved ones might end up hooked to machines or in some other condition that we hoped to avoid. But if we have thought about these issues in advance and are open to the process, at least we won't stand back, paralyzed by discomfort, fear, or ignorance. We will do what we can. We will try. We will make each death, in whatever way we can, a little better.

making decisions

Can life-sustaining medical treatment be withdrawn once it is in place? What if you don't know the patient's wishes? What if she doesn't have a living will? If you stop a particular treatment, are you killing her? Will she suffer? Let's look closely, for a moment, at these questions.

🌿 **Who decides?** Under the law, if a patient is competent, he or she chooses the course of medical care and has the right to refuse any and all treatment, even if that refusal means that the patient will die or suffer needlessly. This bears repeating. *No one can force a treatment upon a patient who doesn't want it.* The patient is in charge. (A patient cannot, however, demand a specific treatment if the doctor considers that treatment to be unwarranted, futile, or unsafe.)

If a patient is not able to make decisions for himself because he cannot understand the choices, communicate his thoughts, or make decisions that are reasonably consistent, a doctor will turn to the family and any advance directives that might be in place for guidance. (As you may recall, advance directives are legal forms that typically include a living will, which states a person's wishes concerning medical care, and a health care proxy, which names someone, usually a family member, to make medical decisions in the patient's stead.)

If a patient is deemed incompetent and has no advance directives, comments he has made to friends and relations should stand as an indication of his wishes, especially if his doctor or several people heard him express his views. In some states, a relative might be assigned to serve as the patient's health care proxy. In a few states, the patient's "best interest," as determined by the state, is used as a guide. The problem is that determining all of this consumes valuable time and emotional energy, which is why it is always best to have the papers in order.

By the way, in some states, artificial nutrition and hydration are not considered extraordinary measures and these treatments cannot be withheld or withdrawn unless the patient has specifically addressed the use of such treatments in his living will. (Because people can become sick and be hospitalized outside of their home state, it's a good idea to include specific instructions about such treatments, regardless of the local protocol.)

Now those are the general rules. In practice, whether there are legal directives or not, most doctors will listen to the patient, even if he or she is only partially cognizant, and will work with all family members to reach some consensus on the course of care. Doctors should heed any instructions the patient has left—oral or written— without exception. But some doctors might disregard those directives if the instructions are vague and family members have views that conflict with the patient's wishes. If there is uncertainty or a dispute between family members or between the doctor and the family, a hospital committee, and if necessary, the court, may intervene.

It is important to reiterate that a patient can refuse any and all medical procedures, and usually, with enough insistence, a family and friends can stop medical treatment. While it is generally more difficult to stop treatment than it is to reject it in the first place, it is possible, it is legal, and it is done routinely. Certainly a round of chemotherapy can be discontinued if it doesn't seem to be helping, but more invasive tools, such as ventilators, dialysis machines, and even feeding tubes can also be withdrawn. Courts have repeatedly upheld the right of patients and their surrogate decision-makers to withdraw treatment.

⚜ **How does one make such decisions?** This is the hard part. How does anyone actually do any of this? First of all, whether you are the patient or the loved one on the sidelines, try to anticipate what lies ahead so you do not end up facing a crisis blindly. As soon as someone becomes seriously ill, or if an elderly relative is frail and failing, ask the doctor what the future might hold—while recognizing that he or she can make only an educated guess. Find out what symptoms are apt to occur in this situation, what medications are likely to be prescribed, what treatment choices might arise, and at what point hospice care might be an option. Once you have this information, discuss the various possibilities and what might be done.

Second, any time you consider a treatment option, define what it is you are trying to accomplish. Are you aiming, first and foremost, to cure an illness? Or are you hoping instead to preserve some level of independence, or to retain a particular ability, such as walking or living independently? Or is your primary goal quality of life and comfort? Most of us blindly choose a treatment because it will fight a disease—an obvious goal—but sometimes it is a futile effort that should be set aside for more obtainable endpoints. Once you know your goal, decisions about specific treatments should become clearer.

Finally, if you want to see if a treatment will help, define "help"— that is, what outcome would qualify as an improvement? Then determine how long you will allow the trial to go on, and decide what you will do if the treatment does not meet the stated goals. Perhaps you've promised your mother that you will never put her on a ventilator, but now a situation has arisen in which it seems like the ventilator might help get her through a brief medical crisis. So you allow her to be put on a ventilator, but with the caveat that if after one week she has not regained consciousness or shown signs of regaining her strength, you will remove the ventilator. Obviously you are not bound by this, but it gives you a goal and a timeline so you are not floating endlessly along, unsure of how or when to change course.

♨ **How does one ever refuse or withdraw treatment for a loved one?** If you are ever in the position of making such decisions for a loved one—and there is a good chance you will be—keep in mind that you are not deciding what *you* want, but what you believe *the patient* would want. These can be polar opposites. Try to ignore your desperate pleas for the person to live, and listen. If your father could speak to you now, what would he tell you to do? What would he say to you? Listen for his voice. Think about who he is, what he valued in life, and what he feared. Once you know what he would want, you only have to find the strength to carry out his wishes.

If possible, take time to be sure of your decision. Get all the information you need. Get a second opinion. Confer with family members and other loved ones. Take time to grieve. Then heed his wishes. Don't be swayed by what others might think; trust yourself.

treatment choices

All sorts of complicated choices can arise at the end of life, but there are some issues and decisions that are frequently involved. It helps to know at least a little bit about them.

❧ **What is life support?** The phrase commonly refers to a ventilator, also known as a respirator, which is a large machine, about the size of a mini-refrigerator, that forces oxygen into the lungs through a tube that is inserted into the nose or mouth or directly into the trachea (windpipe). Being on life support does not necessarily mean someone is dying. People are often put on ventilators, or "intubated," while they recover from surgery or an accident, and then successfully weaned from the machine. However, a patient who is in the late stages of a terminal illness or who is elderly and very frail is not likely to get off the machine and resume breathing independently.

Machines are not nearly as efficient as working bodies, and being on a ventilator is not the same as breathing. The tube is irritating, and the sensation of having air forced into one's lungs is uncomfortable. Also, the ventilator itself is only the beginning. Usually patients who are on a ventilator cannot eat or drink, so they must receive nutrition and hydration artificially, which means more tubes, discomfort, and possible complications. They typically cannot speak. They have to receive medications by tubes. They almost always need a catheter, which is inserted into the bladder. These patients are also under tight medical surveillance; their heart rate, blood pressure, and other vital signs are monitored vigilantly. Because they cannot cough, secretions must be sucked up regularly and the lungs monitored, for there is a possibility of developing an infection. They often have their wrists tied down so they won't dislodge any tubes. And they are typically given sedatives and muscle relaxants to ease the discomfort, so they are not fully alert, if they are alert at all. It's not a pretty scene.

When a patient is seriously ill, especially if he or she has lung disease, it is critical that the patient or the patient's surrogates talk to the doctor about the possibility of life support. In what instances would the patient want to be put on a ventilator, and in what instances would he or she want to forgo such treatment? Is there any real chance that this person would ever get off the respirator and breathe on her own? What would her life be like on a respirator? What can be done to relieve her distress if it is not used?

By the way, when life support is withdrawn, no one actually "pulls a plug"; this is just a coarse way of saying that life-sustaining treatment, usually a ventilator, is being stopped with the understanding that the patient will die soon afterward. While it seems drastic, this death does not have to be painful. In fact, just the opposite is true; death is likely to be far less painful than if the invasive treatment

were continued. The patient should be given painkillers and sedatives in advance and then, once the drugs have taken effect, the ventilator can be removed gradually. Once the tube is removed, the
patient might be given oxygen (through small tubes inserted in the
nostrils) to keep him comfortable. Family members can stay with
the patient, talk to him, hold him, lie with him, or just be near. Sometimes people die immediately after the ventilator is removed; sometimes they continue to breathe for hours or even days on their own.

❧ What are artificial hydration and nutrition? If a patient simply needs fluids, a solution of water, sugar (glucose), and salt is sent
via an intravenous line (IV drip) from a plastic bag that hangs on a
metal rod, down a thin tube, and through a needle into a vein, usually
in the patient's arm or hand. If a patient cannot eat over a period of
time, things get a bit more complicated. For short-term needs (perhaps a week or so), nutrients are often provided through a tube that
goes into the nose and down into the stomach—a technique known as
enteral nutrition. For longer periods, artificial nutrition, or "tube
feeding," may be necessary. In this case, a tube is placed through the
abdominal wall directly into the stomach. If this is not possible
because the gastrointestinal tract is diseased or damaged, nutrients
can be pumped directly into the bloodstream via a catheter (a small
tube) which is inserted into a large vein near the heart. This technique, called total parenteral nutrition, is risky because it can block
blood vessels or cause life-threatening infections.

Artificial nutrition and intravenous hydration raise all sorts of
complex questions primarily because we so misunderstand them.
Although the medical profession as well as the courts consider such
procedures to be medical treatments, many people can't help but
think of food and water as comfort care. They may know a person is

dying, but they don't want him to starve to death or be thirsty. So they hook him to machines and insist that this is not medicine, but love.

The fact is, artificial nutrition and hydration are not the same as eating or drinking. This is not a home-cooked meal eagerly accepted or a refreshing, cool drink of water. These are medical treatments that force nutrients and fluids into a body that cannot drink or eat, and in most cases does not want food or water.

The human body, once it has finished its initial struggle to live, is pretty adept at dying. Most people who are close to death lose their appetites and don't drink more than small sips of fluids. This is because the heart, lungs, kidneys, and other organs are shutting down. The body no longer needs food and water—indeed, it cannot handle food and water. Forcing nutrients and fluids into a body that can no longer digest, circulate, or dispose of them can lead to all sorts of complications including shortness of breath, a backlog of water into the lungs, severe constipation or diarrhea, bloating, and infections. So the effort actually makes the person less comfortable, not more. Furthermore, the tubes themselves are uncomfortable and distance the patient from loved ones. Patients do often feel dryness; swabbing the mouth and lips and moisturizing the skin can bring relief.

Stopping artificial hydration and nutrition once they have been started is not thought to be painful or distressing. Dying patients who moan and grimace because of a wound or painful tumor do not express any such discomfort when they are disconnected from nutrition and hydration devices. They do not appear to suffer from thirst or hunger. In fact, studies suggest that when nutrition and hydration intake is reduced, the body releases larger quantities of endorphins, natural pain-relieving and comfort-inducing chemicals. Dehydration, which causes the patient to lapse into a coma and die peacefully, has even been called "nature's anesthetic."

And yet, some states still consider artificial hydration and nutrition as something special, something separate from other medical treatments, and they require that living wills include specific statements regarding such techniques. In the absence of such written statements, the patient may be forced to receive such care.

🌢 **What are CPR and DNR?** CPR stands for cardiopulmonary resuscitation—*cardio* refers to the heart, and *pulmonary* to the lungs. CPR is performed when a patient's heart or lungs stop working. Outside a medical setting, people perform mouth-to-mouth resuscitation. Air is blown into the patient's mouth, forcing oxygen into the lungs, while someone pushes rhythmically on the heart, trying to keep the blood flowing. Within a medical facility, air is usually provided through a device called an Ambu-bag, and a lifeless heart may be jolted with electrode paddles in an effort to restart it. If the patient survives the attempted resuscitation, he or she is then usually hooked up to a ventilator and other life-sustaining machinery.

When patients are seriously ill or extremely old, CPR is rarely effective. Most don't survive the attempt—which, by the way, is a loud, frantic, and brutal experience—and those who do survive suffer terribly and die soon afterward. The chance of a person surviving CPR outside a hospital is about 15 percent, and "surviving" only means that he lives through the crisis. In a hospital, 45 percent survive the procedure, 15 percent live to leave the hospital, and 5 percent are left in a persistent vegetative state. The odds become even grimmer—in fact pretty close to zero—for patients who are elderly or have a terminal illness. Because of this, severely ill patients often have a DNR, or Do Not Resuscitate, order written into their medical charts. This means that if the patient's breathing or heartbeat stops, hospital staff should not attempt to revive him.

Of course, nothing is simple. Many hospitals now offer a menu of DNR options. For example, a straight DNR might forbid chest compressions to restart the heart, but all other life-sustaining efforts would be allowed. More elaborate versions of the form might be needed to avoid other treatments, such as defibrillation (the use of electric paddles to restart the heart), a ventilator, tube feeding, antibiotics, heart and blood pressure medications, and transfusions. When discussing DNR orders with a doctor, be as specific as possible.

To ensure that a DNR is followed, you will have to talk to any doctors or nurses that care for the patient. Be sure that they understand what is to be done, and not done, under various circumstances. Also, ask what they will do to keep the patient comfortable if a crisis occurs. If the patient is at home, find out how to keep paramedics from attempting resuscitation. Many states recognize at-home DNRs, which might be a document (kept in some visible place, like on the refrigerator), or a bracelet or other identifying accessory. However, unless such documentation exists, paramedics must begin resuscitation efforts. An at-home DNR is important to have even if a patient is under the care of a hospice program because sometimes in an emergency, family members or other caregivers panic and call 911 rather than a hospice nurse.

If you are ever caring for someone who has an at-home DNR, or even someone who has a DNR in the hospital, think about how you might respond in an emergency. Calling 911 or yelling for a nurse to do something is instinctual, so think about what you might do instead, how you might hold the patient and talk to him or her, and say your good-byes.

⚘ If a patient has a living will, does he need a DNR too? Yes. Living wills simply outline what medical treatments a person would or would not want if he were near death and unable to make decisions for himself. They are written in advance, often well in advance, of any dire situation and the instructions are typically quite general. Health care professionals may or may not give the document much credence, and are not likely to even consider it in an emergency unless a family member is at the bedside with the document in hand and screaming frantically. A DNR, on the other hand, is a medical order issued by a physician regarding specific treatments that are not to be used on a patient who is already extremely ill and is not expected to survive the resuscitation attempt or is not expected to do well despite any such attempts.

⚜ **What is a "persistent vegetative state"? What is a coma? What is "brain death"?** Once upon a time if a heart was beating and lungs were drawing in air, a person was considered to be alive. If these things were not happening, he was dead. It was a simple concept. Then machines were developed that could keep blood and oxygen and nutrition circulating, so a string of new terms were coined, such as "persistent vegetative state" and "brain death." These terms describe a growing twilight zone between life and death, where people linger, one foot in this world, one foot in another, not quite alive but not fully, or seemingly, dead. For families who must feel their way across this dark landscape, weighed down by doubts and sorrow, it is a baffling and extraordinarily painful place to be.

A patient in a coma is like someone under heavy anesthesia or in a very deep sleep. Most of the brain is out of order, but enough of it works so that the patient might, for example, breathe on his own. A coma may be the result of any number of problems, including a head injury, brain tumor, severe stroke, drug overdose, or uncontrolled diabetes. People often come out of comas and resume relatively normal lives. However, once in a deep coma for any length of time (say, more than a couple of months), the odds of recovery drop precipitously and a patient enters what is known as a persistent vegetative state. At this point, most of the brain function is gone. The only part of the brain that is functioning is the brain stem, a little bulb at the top of the spinal cord that regulates rudimentary bodily functions, such as breathing, heart rate, wake-sleep cycles, body temperature, waste elimination, and some reflexive movements. Very, very few people come out of this state, and none recover fully.

For loved ones, it is a bewildering nightmare. The patient is lying there, breathing, coughing, jerking, blinking, yawning. His eyes may roam around the room. His lips may even curl into a smile. And yet, despite all these signs of human life, sophisticated scanners show that patients in persistent vegetative states do not think, register emotions, or feel pain. They are bodies, living shells, and little more. The chance of regaining consciousness is almost zero, but not precisely zero—a tiny but torturous gap. With skilled medical care and life support, patients can be kept alive in this condition for years.

The expression "brain death," as well as terms like "biological death" and "clinical death," is more a cruel linguistic trick than a physical state. "Brain death" means death. The entire brain has stopped functioning. The brain is dead. The person is dead. The only difference between "brain death" and "death" is that in the former, drugs and machines might be used to keep the heart beating and oxygen circulating, and if the spinal cord is intact, there may be some reflexive movement.

"Brain death" is a ridiculous term because it suggests that some part of the body is still alive. Family and other loved ones see the person lying on a bed, his skin is still soft and warm, and so they feel that he is, at least on some level, alive. *We understand his brain is dead, but how is the rest of him doing, Doc?* It seems that he is only in a deep sleep, a coma, or some other state from which he could awaken. But it simply isn't so. The patient is legally and biologically dead. These terms are useful for physicians who may want to certify death but mechanically keep the heart and lungs functioning so that organs can be donated. But they are disturbing for families who may be haunted by doubts and unsure of what's really happening.

the possibilities

making the passage richer

Typically, when a doctor knows that death is inevitable, that all the drugs or surgery or radiation in the world cannot stop this process, he or she turns grimly toward the patient and/or family and says, "I'm sorry. There is nothing more that we can do."

This is a travesty. These words should be outlawed from hospitals, banned from nursing homes, erased from our lexicon. What a horrible thing to say, and what a profound untruth it is. For it is now, when death is inescapable, that there is so very much to be done, and doctors should help direct families toward that work. In fact, the patient and loved ones should have been encouraged to start this work long before this point.

What is to be done and how it is done, through gestures large or small, will depend on the patient, the family, and friends. A patient might want to set some priorities, and, if it is not already too late, act on them. He or she might want to take a long-desired trip, write letters, give away treasured belongings, get in touch with long-lost friends, or say anything that needs to be said—*I'm sorry. I love you. You are forgiven.* This is a time to be kind to oneself—to allow the tears and emotional pain, to acknowledge the very human needs and fears that arise, and to refuse any blame for what is happening. Most important, it is a time to surround oneself with family and friends.

No one should be thinking, much less saying, "There is nothing more we can do." It is this sort of attitude that leaves family members grief-stricken and numb, staring silently, waiting, and watching. They have been told there is nothing more to be done, and so they do nothing. But they desperately want to do *something*. Inertia is of no value to the patient and leaves family members and other loved ones feeling powerless, useless, and anxious. This helplessness, this inability to soothe and comfort a loved one at such a time, is often more upsetting for survivors than anything else. And it is often what drives families to push for more therapies.

Betty Lou Muhlfeld was adamant that she not receive aggressive life-sustaining care at the end of her life. She had watched both her mother and her sister struggle with cancer, undergo surgery, radiation, and chemotherapy, and then die long and agonizing deaths, and it was not going to happen to her. She was not going to be disfigured, debilitated, or immobilized. "She was a person who absolutely loved life and lived it to its fullest," her daughter Lucy said. "She didn't like growing old. And she felt that there was no desperate urge to continue if life were no longer fun. She would say, 'If I become incapacitated, just kill me.'"

In her late sixties, Betty Lou was diagnosed with breast cancer. She had her breast removed and seemed to be cured. Ten years later, the cancer apparently returned. No one knows for sure what happened because she never sought medical care and was never diagnosed. But she seemed to know that the cancer was back, and she did nothing to stop it. During the last year of her life, she reminded her daughters that she did not want aggressive treatment, and asked them, if it were ever necessary, if they would help her kill herself.

Unfortunately, that was pretty much all that was said. There was no plan for exactly how this quick, clean death might occur. Without a diagnosis, much less a prognosis, hospice could not step in, and no other home-care agency or doctor was in a position to carry out her wishes—to help her die when they didn't even know what was wrong with her. So when Betty Lou had trouble swallowing one evening, her family did the only thing they could: they took her to the emergency room. Doctors discovered that her intestinal tract was blocked. They wove a tube through her nose and into her stomach so they could continually pump out its contents (since nothing could get through the other way). They began artificial feeding and hydration. And they recommended a colostomy—surgery in which part of the large intestine is pulled through a permanent opening in the belly and feces are discharged directly into a bag. Now, Betty Lou had no intention of having a colostomy. Her mother had had one and this was the one procedure she never wanted to endure. But the doctors insisted that the blockage might be due to something treatable—maybe it was not cancer, but some benign intestinal disorder—and without treatment, she would, in one doctor's words, "explode." Her children coaxed and she finally acquiesced. "She said, 'This is not what I want, but I'll do it,'" Lucy recalled.

Betty Lou awoke after her surgery to find not only a colostomy bag attached to her belly, but a breathing tube blocking her mouth. "It horrified her," Lucy said. The blockage, as it turned out, was cancerous, and although her doctors thought they might be able to extend her life, maybe by several years, Betty Lou had no interest in pursuing chemotherapy or radiation treatments. So they removed the feeding tube, and gave her morphine. Eight days after her surgery, Betty Lou died.

Lucy is sad that her mother suffered, that she had a stomach pump, feeding tube, breathing tube, monitors, and surgery, but she recognizes that her family had little choice, given that they didn't know what was wrong with Betty Lou and thought, quite reasonably, that she might have survived with treatment. What she really regrets, what pains her deeply, is not the tubes or surgery her mother endured. What makes her cry anew when she recalls those final days is that she didn't know how to talk to her mother, how to calm her, cheer her, and say good-bye. Even once she knew without doubt that her mother was dying, she didn't know how to fill those final days of living, how to give her mother the kind of celebratory send-off that she deserved and would have loved.

"We were all gathered around, staring at her for twenty-four hours a day," Lucy recalled. "She would open her eyes and look up and just see us all staring at her and rubbing her arms. I think it must have been horrifying, or embarrassing. . . . I couldn't say anything. I didn't talk to her. I just stared.

"I wish that I had spoken to her about death and how she was feeling. I wish I had asked her, 'Are you scared? How can I help you through this?'. . . If we had all had scotch-and-sodas in our hands and we had brought in a family album and she could have heard us telling old stories, there's no question that would have given her such pleasure.

"You're sitting there and you, you just want to send all your energies, you want to, to soak them up . . . ," Lucy said, unable to finish her sentence. She cried for a moment and then continued. "I think I'll do it better next time. Maybe. I know now that it's all right to laugh, to talk about wonderful things, and to be joyful and happy. Let's face it, we all know what's happening in that room. So rather than sit there like some cloud, staring, why not make it a little more soothing and joyful?"

Whatever is going on medically, this final stage of someone's life is not a time to be sitting "like some cloud." It is a time of the greatest heights of human love and the deepest depths of human agony. It is a time of dying, but it is also, more than ever before, a time for living.

I offer a few examples here to give you a sense of what is possible. But each person is different. While touch is a powerful relaxant for one person, it can make another tense. One person might be open to shared meditation, while another squirms at the mere thought of it.

🌿 **Hospice care.** The sole purpose of hospice programs is to help people live fully and die peacefully, and hospices are wonderfully adept at doing that. The goal of hospice care is not to fight death, but to make the most of life, by keeping the patient as comfortable and able as possible, and by helping him to find peace in his relationships and his life. While families provide most of the hands-on care, hospice staff provide medical, psychological, spiritual, and practical support both to the patients and their families.

Hospice care is not about giving up or waiting to die. It is not "soft" medicine, nor is it outside the bounds of conventional medicine. People who use hospice services receive superior medical treatment from top-notch doctors, nurses, and other professionals. The only difference is that the aim of treatment is comfort, and everyone's energy is focused on living life, not on fighting death.

The term "hospice" is a bit confusing because in some places, such as Great Britain, where the hospice movement first became popular, hospices are small medical facilities where patients live. In other countries, hospices are homes for the destitute. In America, the word hospice refers not to bricks and mortar, but to a philosophy of care and a program of services. While some American hospices care for patients within a free-standing unit or a special wing of a hospital or nursing home, most provide services to patients who live at home. Nurses and social workers visit the patient and family as needed. Home health aides and volunteers often spend several hours each day in the patient's home. But beyond this, most of the day-to-day care falls on the family.

There are thousands of hospice organizations across the United States and Canada. The programs are accessible to most people. However, hospice is a philosophy of care that can be adopted even if no formal program exists nearby; it just takes legwork and a strong commitment to such care. Home-care agencies that are not certified hospices can often provide hospice-type care if you round up the right team.

Hospice care is hobbled by the fact that Medicare and other insurance plans require a doctor to declare that a patient has less than six months to live—a prediction doctors are hard-pressed to make. They can prognosticate with some confidence when it comes to many forms of cancer—although even that is getting more difficult as new treatments are developed—but it is difficult to make such a call for patients with less predictable illnesses such as heart and vascular disease, chronic lung disease, or dementia.

Doctors are also often reluctant to suggest hospice care because they don't want to upset the patient and family. Or they might hold out hope of turning things around, despite what they know about the prognosis. Or they might think they can provide adequate palliative care, without realizing how complex and time-consuming such care can be.

Sometimes people do not receive hospice care because there is no inpatient unit nearby and family members and friends cannot provide, or have no interest in providing, the kind of physical and emotional care that is required to keep someone who is terminally ill at home.

But one of the biggest obstacles to hospice care is that people are not ready, not prepared either emotionally or mentally, to choose that route. As things stand now, hospice is an all-or-nothing choice. Almost all hospice programs insist that patients forgo all life-sustaining medical treatment. A patient might receive radiation to shrink a tumor or surgery to clear a blockage if that treatment will make the patient more comfortable. But in most cases, a patient would not receive any treatment aimed solely at fighting the underlying disease, largely because such treatments can get in the way of comfort care and the emotional work of dying, but also because hospices are not reimbursed for such procedures. This means that patients and their families must make a tremendous leap in their thinking—a leap many are not ready to make.

Patients and their families, as well as their doctors, often don't want to believe that the patient will die. They don't want to let go, they don't want to accept death. Not yet. Not now. When I asked the daughter-in-law of a man who was clearly dying whether the family had considered hospice care, she responded with disgust, "He doesn't want to just sit and wait and *die*." No, she explained, the family was looking into other possible treatments for him. Her father-in-law died two days after our conversation.

If you or someone you love is ever seriously ill and hospice care is of any interest, don't wait until the last minute to get in touch with a program. Even if it does not seem to be time for hospice yet, or if you think you may not even need hospice, initiate a conversation, learn about the local program, and discuss the patient's situation with staff members. That way, you will have some introduction to the services, and if and when such care needed, all the players will be in place. (To learn about the local hospice or to get a referral, ask a doctor, visit the National Hospice and Palliative Care Web site at www.nhpc.org, or call the Hospice Helpline at 800-658-8898 or the Hospice Association of America at 202-546-4759.)

⚘ **Palliative care.** For those patients who remain in the hospital, comfort care is often still possible, it's just a whole lot more difficult to get. More and more hospitals are establishing palliative care programs, and others are becoming more aware of such services.

When an illness is being aggressively treated, pain and symptoms are often unavoidable. The disease causes pain, the treatments can cause pain, and the effort to treat the disease can preclude the use of high doses of pain medication, as such medication can cause drowsiness and can compromise certain bodily functions, such as respiration. But certainly hospital patients could be made more comfortable than they are. And once someone switches tracks from aggressive treatment of disease to palliative care—which is aimed not at curing disease or even fending off death, but at improving the comfort and quality of the patient's life—pain can be eased dramatically. In fact, palliative care experts claim that almost all dying patients can be kept relatively comfortable.

But palliative care is a relatively new field of medicine and the techniques involved in pain management, much less the more comprehensive art of psychological, social, and spiritual care, are not widely known. Perhaps more to the point, in a busy hospital where the goal is to make people better, palliative care is simply not a priority, and tasks aimed merely at keeping patients comfortable are overlooked. Patients routinely fail to receive adequate medical attention for pain, nausea, and other symptoms, and hospital personnel do not have the time to explore nonmedical approaches to pain, such as relaxation techniques, music, psychological and spiritual counseling, gentle massage, and the presence and support of loved ones.

In the hospital, patients tend to get pulled along with the current, and a strong current it is. You, as the patient or as a loved one, will have to fight for the kind of treatment you want. You will have to talk to the doctor and any nurses involved. If you do not want all-out, life-saving medical care, you'll have to make clear what your goals and expectations are, perhaps by posting signs above the patient's bed that explain what is to be done—and not done—in an emergency, and list the priorities for care (i.e., comfort, peace, time with friends and family, etc.). Hospitals are not set up to provide good end-of-life care, but things are improving, and with an assertive effort, you might find some reasonable amount of comfort and peace.

🌿 **Pain medications.** Doctors tend to be stingy with pain medications because they erroneously fear legal action, because they worry that the medications are not safe in large doses, and because they have their own biases and misconceptions. Sometimes doctors wonder if a particular patient isn't just or complaining unnecessarily. Sometimes they are concerned about patients becoming addicted to such drugs. Sometimes they want to avoid the confusion and drowsiness these drugs can cause, or worry about hastening death through the use of narcotics. The truth is that a) if a patient says she is in pain, she is in pain—her own perception of pain is adequate evidence that pain exists; b) people who are not prone to addiction will not become addicts because they are given narcotic painkillers (and anyway, who cares about addiction when someone is dying?); and c) while confusion must be weighed when administering drugs, the patient should be the guide in determining how to balance pain and sedation.

Patients are to blame as well. Some believe that "good" patients don't complain, that "good" patients are stoic and quiet. Some feel that they are "giving in" to a disease if they take pain medication. Some worry about side effects or worry that if they take the medication early in their disease, the drugs won't work later when the pain is more severe. And sometimes they believe, in this era of "just say no," that morphine and other narcotics are dangerous and should be avoided.

Pain should be treated, and it should be treated aggressively. Doing so does not alter the course of an illness, limit the effectiveness of future pain management, suggest anything about the character of a patient, or create drug addicts. Pain, as I've already mentioned, is permeating. It changes our personalities, making us short-tempered, tired, and less able to cope or interact with others. It leads to other symptoms, such as anxiety, depression, nausea, and insomnia. And chronic pain makes people less able to cope with any pain, so small aches can feel monstrous.

Ideally, medication is given at regular intervals, *before* pain becomes acute and, therefore, harder to control. Doses should escalate to match the pain. And finally, other methods, such as nerve blocks, should be explored.

Without the help of a hospice program or a palliative care expert, you will have to be knowledgeable, determined, and perhaps even a bit belligerent to get adequate pain relief for yourself or your loved one. Go ahead, be noisy. Demand that pain and any other symptoms be treated.

Having said all this, it is important to note that narcotics, sedatives, and other medications are only one element of comfort care. Alternative medicine offers other useful tools to combat pain and anxiety, such as acupuncture, reflexology, meditation, and relaxation techniques. And emotional, spiritual, and family support is absolutely essential. No one should be stingy with pain medications, but morphine should not take the place of spiritual support, and sedatives should not be given in lieu of gentle reassurances and tender touch. We must not numb the body and then neglect the soul, for suffering at the end of life extends well beyond physical discomfort, and dying well involves far more than dying free of pain.

♨ **"Double effect."** When people talk of a "double effect," they are referring to the belief that giving morphine in doses hefty enough to keep a dying person comfortable will not only kill the pain, but may also kill the patient. Family members are often left feeling that, in their effort to ensure the patient's comfort, they have actually caused his or her death. Proponents of physician-assisted suicide also use the notion of "double effect" to support their position. Doctors, they argue, sometimes prescribe large doses of morphine with the dual effect (and, in some cases, dual purpose) of easing pain and hastening death, so why not legalize this activity and let them kill patients without any other objective? This gets into a lengthy debate about intent—death as a side effect of treatment versus death as a goal of treatment. But what has been overlooked and underreported is the fact that no one has ever proven that increasingly large doses of morphine can kill patients or even alter the course of an illness. In fact, there is evidence that morphine, given palliatively, does *not* contribute to death. (And some research suggests that it may actually help to prolong life.)

It is true that morphine acts on the breathing center in the brain and, under normal circumstances, large doses of it can compromise respiration and cause death. However, researchers are now finding that if morphine is given in moderate doses that are increased gradually, as is done with terminally ill patients, those doses can be pushed well beyond what would normally be a deadly quota, and not have a fatal effect. Apparently, the respiratory system becomes tolerant of the drug and can withstand incredibly large quantities of it—ten times the dose normally given to cancer patients—doses that would kill someone who had not built up such tolerance.

⚜ **Gathering friends and family.** Whether someone is at home with hospice, or in an ICU, this is a time to be with family and dear friends. (A good tale: A woman reached a ripe old age and sent invitations to all her friends to come to her "funeral." She explained that most of them would get together when she died and she did not want to miss such a gathering, so she was having her funeral early. They could come now, and they wouldn't have to come later. And so, she had a joyous time with all her friends at her own "funeral" just a year before she actually died.)

Once someone is bedridden, the mere presence of loved ones is often all that is necessary. You don't need to involve the patient in conversation; just having a few special people nearby, talking to each other, telling stories, reading aloud, or just sitting quietly, can offer the dying person enormous comfort.

⚜ **Forgiveness and healing.** This is also, among other things, a time of closure. It is a time of finishing the unfinished. As much as possible, mistakes need to be forgiven, wounds healed, severed relationships repaired.

Sometimes people worry that if they proffer their love or forgiveness they will make the whole thing seem too serious. Better to err on the side of being too forgiving and too loving, if there is such a thing. If the patient goes through a particularly serious setback and then recovers, that is a perfect time to tell him that you were worried and the experience made you realize that you had thoughts that needed to be aired.

However, it is also important to note that just because you need to reconcile the relationship doesn't mean that you will be able to. The person who is dying may not have the interest in or strength for such matters. Say what you need to say, but don't be angry if your loved one can't or won't respond. They heard you. Let it go.

⚜ **Creating legacies.** When people realize that life is coming to a close they often want to leave something behind, something that reflects their life, their history, or their values. A legacy represents some facet of a person—his ancestry, his hobbies, his thoughts, his dreams. Creating a legacy is a powerful tool, helping people to pass something of value on to others and begin the process of letting go. For survivors, the gift, whether it be elaborate or whimsical, is a lasting and meaningful remembrance of this person's life and spirit. Something to cherish, read, or review. Something to make them cry, laugh, or simply remember.

There are any number of ways to create a legacy: write letters, keep a journal, assemble a photo album, give away jewelry or trinkets, draw up a family tree, paint, make a video- or audiotape recording, dictate a story. Or a person might plant a special garden or write poetry or make a collage. Of course, you can always do these things now in life, rather than waiting for some terminal illness.

♠ **Reminiscing and life review.** Reviewing one's life can help a person realize that her life was, indeed, valuable, and that despite any mistakes that were made, she has accomplished many things, small and large. It allows her to pass on family history and it returns her to better times, moments that were fun or meaningful, times when she was happy and carefree and strong.

While people often do their own internal life review, loved ones can help the process by asking questions, or discussing special moments. (You might want to tape-record or videotape this conversation.) Through this, they not only help the patient, but they stand to learn things about this person—how Mom met Dad, who her ancestors were, the fact that she used to spend all her free time painting—things that they might not have a chance to learn later.

Ask about your father's childhood, his playmates, his parents and grandparents, and his early schooldays. What did his childhood house look like? Was he rebellious as a teenager? What were the most memorable moments in his life? What was his first job? What did he like most or least about his last job? And so on.

When a person can no longer talk, you can help revive these good times for him. When my father was dying, my mother, siblings, and I talked often about the wonderful things we had done together, reminding him that he had had a good life and was a good father, while also pulling his mind into pleasant scenes. We recalled the way he would stand at the edge of the pool, holding his nose and waiting nonchalantly for one of us little ones to push him in, or how he would carry us on his shoulders and swerve around as if he were going to drop us at any minute. At one point, when he was almost unconscious, I softly sang the school song of the university that he and I had both attended—a school he had loved dearly—and as I came to the refrain, his eyes popped open and he sang loudly along with me, even finding the energy for a few hand motions. It's a sweet memory for me.

We also talked in some detail about his favorite places, and in doing so, took him once again to those places. As my father lay dying, we strolled together along California beaches, we sailed along the coast of Maine, we walked along the rocky, pine-covered paths behind our summer cottage. As we described these familiar sights and sounds, his body relaxed as it floated freely away from his sickness and reentered these beloved places. Or maybe, he became them. For me, my father is not only in these places now, he has become part of them. He is the glowing sunset over Big Sur; the stony bridge he built, rock by rock, on a tranquil Canadian lake; the waves lapping rhythmically against the side of our friend Ralph Halsey's sailboat. He is, as a wave or a sail or a rock, serene, and always there for me.

⚜ **Spiritual support.** Even people who have not been spiritual in life often become attuned to spirituality and religion in the face of death. Offering spiritual support is not about administering last rites or a perfunctory meeting with a member of the clergy. It is about listening to and exploring a person's deepest questions, fears, and needs, and discovering what gives them strength and comfort. It might mean religious discussions or readings, but it also might mean something different altogether. Our job is to be open to it and to allow it, accepting spirituality in a variety of guises.

Douglas C. Smith, in his book *Caregiving*, tells wonderful stories about people who found spirituality in religion, in magic, in what some might dismiss as hallucinations, and even in thinking about a favorite bar. It is important that we not impose our own beliefs on others, but remain open to an individual's own form of spirituality and allow it to provide the person who is dying with some comfort.

✿ **Relaxation techniques.** There are a number of ways to help someone relax, which can help ease not only stress or fear, but also physical pain. These are useful to learn for any stressful situation, and it's helpful to have them in place so they are familiar when illness is a factor. In one method, you lead the person's mind toward a soothing place, somewhat as I did with my father. In another method, you focus not on the place and the memories, but on the body's response to the place and the physical release it inspires. Most often, a beach is described. Speaking in a soft and even voice, describe tension flowing out of the body and the muscles relaxing one by one as the person eases himself down onto the sand. The warmth of the sun on his chest and face, the rhythmic roar of the ocean as it rolls up onto the shore, the softness of the breeze, the sweet smell of sea air. Talk the person through this exercise, mentioning each muscle of the body, helping them to feel the heaviness, the pull of the sand on each part of the body—toes, ankles, calves, knees, thighs, and so on.

Meditation is also a powerful tool for alleviating stress and pain. Although it is helpful if a person has practiced it in the past, anyone can try it. The person sits comfortably (preferably upright, but a lounging position, or even lying flat is fine), with her eyes closed. She takes a deep breath and then exhales, slowly releasing tension with each breath, focusing on various body parts, one at a time, releasing tension from her toes, feet, calves, and so on, and moving on up to the head. Often people will repeat a word, or mantra, like "peace" or "relax" or "comfort," or any other word that is calming.

✿ **Touch and massage.** Touch is an important element in end-of-life care that we often neglect, so afraid are we of hurting this fragile body, so obstructed by the tubes, so unsure of our place in this event. But the most simple physical contact—stroking a person's arm or combing her hair—can be extraordinarily comforting at this time. Talk to the doctor or nurse. Find out what sort of massage is okay. (Patients can be prone to fractures and blood-clotting, so any rubbing must be gentle.)

🌿 **The sounds that surround.** When all the other senses are off-duty, or fading away, hearing can become surprisingly acute. Anyone who has laid in bed at night listening to the drip, drip, drip of a faucet, or the snoring of a mate, or the buzzing of a meandering fly knows this is true. When a person is dying, hearing is usually the last sense to go. Even when people can't communicate or respond in any way, often they can hear exactly what is said to them right up to the end. They may not comprehend every word, but they can certainly grasp the tone and tenor. This can be unpleasant if a patient must listen to people who are arguing or machines that are beeping or a neighbor who is moaning. But hearing can also be an avenue for profound comfort.

When caring for someone who is gravely ill, remember the importance of sound. Just the ring of familiar voices can bring enormous comfort and relief. When serious illness strikes a loved one, don't sit glumly or talk about the patient as if he were not present. Read aloud. Tell stories. Converse comfortably and naturally with each other. If no one is near, soothing music or even the sound of certain television shows might offer diversion and relief.

🌿 **The joy of laughter.** When we visit someone who is sick, we tend to be solemn to reflect the severity of the situation. Humor seems not only out of place, but irreverent, disrespectful. But humor is just what the doctor ordered, and according to surveys of dying patients, it is what the patient wants too. Most patients say they would rather have their caregivers be humorous than serious. Quite literally, they want to die laughing. Our somber voices and grave faces further distance the patient from the joy of life and the comfort of friends. Whereas humor—not self-conscious humor that is used to hide our awkwardness, but genuine, joyous, unbridled humor—is uplifting and fortifying. It makes people feel alive, easy, and close to others.

There was much humor in our house when my father lay dying. He was terribly funny—slipping puns into our conversation and making faces at our comments—and we were constantly laughing about one thing or another. I think we had run out of other emotions. The laughter also gave us strength, providing some sanity in an utterly insane situation. Sometimes people would call, very serious and sad, and there would be so much laughter in the background that whoever answered the phone had to cup the phone so the caller wouldn't hear what was going on. I am sure some of them thought we had lost it. Which I guess we had. Late one night, when my father could no longer speak, we lay on his bed and sprawled on the floor beside him, watching Mary Tyler Moore reruns and laughing so hard we were gasping for air. I can't imagine a better sound for my father to hear.

♣ **A time of growth and grief.** Besides benefiting the patient, the time together, the reminiscing, the physical care, the laughter, and any headway that is made toward love and forgiveness is potent drink for the survivors, who have a scorching path of grief ahead of them. The more involved they are in the person's dying, the easier the grieving process will be, and the potential for growth will be the greatest.

"Just as the dying can 'grow' even as they die, so can those who tend them so lovingly," Dr. Derek Doyle, the medical director of St. Columba's Hospice in Edinburgh, says in his book *Caring for a Dying*

Relative: A Guide for Families. "They, too, can learn and grow and, in years to come, look back on their time with satisfaction in what they managed to do and wonder at what they learned. Perhaps they saw love in a new light or realized how petty were most of life's squabbles; perhaps they learned about understanding and reconciliation, of sacrificial caring and of the immense strengths we all have within us, so often untapped and untested. . . . When we accept this challenge of caring for the dying, we are not merely doing our duty. . . . We are dedicating ourselves to love in action—ready to receive as much as to give, prepared to learn and even change and be changed."

putting ink to paper

a review of legal documents

No legal form by itself, no matter how cleverly it is written, will protect you from a dreadful death. As we have seen, advance directives
are widely ignored. Even when people list specific treatments that
are to be avoided, they often end up getting just the kind of medical
care they said they did not want. But this does not mean that you
shouldn't bother signing such documents. You absolutely should sign
them—the sooner, the better. It simply means that they alone are not
enough. They must be accompanied by information and thoughtful,
ongoing discussion. So get ahold of the paperwork, sign it, and make
sure your proxy and your doctor each have a copy and understand
your views. Just be sure you do the other work as well.

You can get advance directives, valid in your home state—as well as documents from any other states in which you spend significant time—from Partnership for Caring (formerly known as Choice in Dying), 800-989-9455 or at www.choices.org. You can also get a "Will to Live" from the National Right to Life Committee at 202-626-8800 or www.nrlc.org. Unlike a living will, which usually indicates that a person does not want invasive treatments at a certain point, the Will to Live expresses a person's desire to be kept alive using whatever means possible.

Be sure to choose a medical proxy who knows you well, whom you trust implicitly, and who will listen carefully to your views. It should be someone who would spend time talking with doctors and considering the options carefully, who could communicate effectively with others in the family, and who could make these sorts of monumental decisions on your behalf.

Add any details that you deem to be important to your advance directives, but avoid the urge to be overly specific. You don't want to tie your proxy's hands. As you will see in the next section, while it is important to give ample information about your general goals and desires, you need to leave your proxy with some latitude so he can make decisions that both fit your goals and make sense given a particular situation. Remember, these documents are primarily for legal purposes; most guidance and instruction should occur through conversation with your proxy.

the medical directive

In the 1980s, when it first became clear that the standard living will was not having the desired impact, a number of groups and individuals drafted more detailed documents. One that received quite a bit of attention was a "Medical Directive" proposed by Drs. Ezekiel and Linda Emanuel from Massachusetts General Hospital. The highlight of the Medical Directive is a chart. Across the top are four medical scenarios: a patient in a coma with no hope of recovery; a patient in a coma with a "small likelihood" of recovery but a "much larger likelihood" of dying; a patient with terminal illness and severe, irreversible brain damage; and finally, a patient with severe, irreversible brain damage but no terminal illness. Down the left side of the chart are twelve medical procedures: major surgery, dialysis, antibiotics, chemotherapy, and so on. The idea is that you check off what you would want, would not want, or might like to try, given each scenario.

The Medical Directive is more specific than the living will, but it still doesn't solve the murky issues of language and intent. Does "recovery" refer to total recovery or any recovery at all? What chance of recovery would be considered "a small likelihood" at such a time? And how close to death must a person be to be considered "terminal?" As for the signer's intention, how are we to know what a spouse or parent or friend was thinking when he checked off "I do not want" to antibiotics, to mechanical breathing, to minor surgery? Did he not want those treatments under any circumstances? Did he understand fully what a shunt or a colostomy or a round of antibiotics might mean in some specific situation?

The Medical Directive also includes only four scenarios and twelve treatment options—a very limited menu. Of course, there is no way to catalog all possible end-of-life situations, much less to imagine the treatments or research protocols that will be available in the future. Nor is it possible to include all the uncertainties that are inherent in any medical choice, or the personal issues that color our decisions. For example, the document describes the patient with brain damage as "unable to recognize people or to speak understand-ably," but how is one supposed to proceed if a person has passing moments of lucidity? What if the brain damage appears to be irre-versible, but no one knows that with certainty? What if the patient had heated words with her husband shortly before she had a stroke and he wants to try to pull her back, if just for a moment, so that he can say "I'm sorry"?

Even if a directive were expanded to include more scenarios and issues and treatment choices, there is some question as to whether a person can really give detailed medical instructions in advance. How does anyone, in a healthy or relatively healthy state, know exactly what treatments he or she would want in some theoretical situation? Certainly, you have a general idea. You might know that you wouldn't want to be kept alive by machines if you were barely conscious and had no hope of recovery. You might be able to say with certainty that you consider artificial nutrition as invasive medical treatment, not comfort care. But can you say for sure that you wouldn't want to try a ventilator even for a brief time, that you wouldn't want a blood transfusion, or that you wouldn't want to undergo any surgery at all, even if that surgery might make you more comfortable as you were dying?

Furthermore, as death grows near, a person's opinions about treat-ment might change; indeed, they might change quite radically. After all, we change our minds about what we want for dinner—we cer-tainly might change our minds about what medical treatments we want at the end of life. At such a moment, a person is likely to see the world through a different lens, viewing pain and medical odds and debility through a prism of grief, shock, pain, love, and denial. He might be willing to endure more pain or disability than he had previ-ously imagined, he might be willing to shoot for slimmer odds, or he might want to stop the struggle sooner than he had thought.

When asked about this, Dr. Foley, the palliative care specialist, tells the story of a patient with advanced cancer who was very involved in the Hemlock Society, an organization which advocates the rights of patients to end their own lives and provides them with instructions on how to do so. This woman was absolutely determined to control her death. Her husband had a supply of pills that would kill her, and he had made a pact with her that he would give them to her when the time came. At one point in the course of her illness, the woman was in a lot of pain and only getting sicker, when her kidneys began to fail. Dr. Foley said to her, "This is a time when you could die and it's a wonderful way to die because it's quiet and it's painless and you get sleepy." It seemed to be an obvious choice for such a person. But the woman insisted that the doctors perform surgery to insert little mesh tubes into her kidneys so they would drain properly. Just as Dr. Foley had predicted, after the operation the woman's pain was so severe that she had to be heavily sedated, leaving her very confused and disoriented. Now she was dying exactly as she had always said she didn't want to die: with aggressive and painful medical care aimed at stopping a disease that could not be stopped. "I said to her husband, 'Do you want me to discontinue her feedings? Do you want to discontinue her antibiotics?'" Dr. Foley says. "And he said, 'Oh no, no, no. I only wanted to do that if she was suffering. But she's not suffering now.'"

We cannot choreograph our deaths in advance, ticking off a list of medical instructions for some unknown future event—an event which is likely to be far more murky and chaotic than anything we imagined, an event which is likely to include issues we never anticipated. If we are seriously ill and we know what choices are going to arise, we should be able to craft a fairly reliable plan for our future care. But it is difficult, if not impossible, to pick and choose exactly which treatments we will want and which we won't before any specific question is raised, before we are even sick. How are we to imagine the medical options and odds, the personal issues that might arise, our response to pain, or the value of life at such a time? More important, what are our loved ones to do when they have been told "Don't ever . . . ," and then we open our weary eyes briefly and mumble "yes" to that very treatment? What are they to do with our instructions if they feel, for one reason or another, that a particular treatment should be tried?

value history forms

In response to these concerns, various experts have drafted "value history forms," which include questions about medical treatments, but also ask general questions about a person's views about life and death, his priorities and beliefs. Because it's so difficult to give specific medical instructions, these forms attempt to uncover a person's overall values and intentions so that when the time comes, the specific decisions can be made within the broader context of a person's goals.

This represents a step in the right direction. However, keep in mind that these forms, too, are just pieces of paper, tempting us, yet again, to squeeze a very complicated process into a simple checklist. *I don't want to be in pain. I want my loved ones near. I want to feel safe and secure. I want to be treated with respect.* Who wouldn't agree to all of this? But does it really give a health care proxy all the information he needs when hard questions are on the table and decisions have to be made?

Although the authors of these various documents all emphasize the importance of discussion, the mere presence of these forms, the ease with which they can be completed, suggests that we can handle death as we do so many other things in our busy lives: with a quick fix. A five-step diet plan, a no-sweat exercise routine, a twenty-minute power lunch, and a two-page document directing the final passage of our lives.

Value history forms and other similar documents are useful to look through, complete, and use as a springboard for conversations with your loved ones. But on their own, they are, quite often, not enough.

a letter of love

In addition to any directives, it's a good idea to write a letter that reiterates and clarifies what was said in any conversations. While your directives provide legal documentation of your wishes, a letter provides your proxy and other loved ones with additional guidance and support during this terrible time. It is your voice, whispering in their ears, as they wrestle with how to proceed and anguish over your loss.

A letter might, for example, express your sorrow that your loved ones are having to make such decisions and your gratitude to them for caring for you in this way. It might raise a few issues for them to think about while they are making this decision, and then relieve them of any feelings of responsibility they might be left with. It may or may not change what they do, but it is a gentle and familiar hand on their shoulders, a reassuring embrace, letting them know that they are doing the right thing.

Even if you never finish this letter, trying to write it is a good exercise, as it forces you to think about what is important to you and what you want your proxy to know. What would matter to you at such a time? What do you want your loved ones to consider? What do you want to say to them?

You might find yourself getting a bit tearful, sitting there before that blank page or staring at the computer screen, thinking in frighteningly realistic terms about the passing of your life, the good-byes, and the feelings of those you leave behind. But these are good tears, useful tears, and your words, if you can find them, will be a source of great comfort to those who one day must read them.

jean's story

Jean-Roland Coste, who died of AIDS at the terribly young age of 33, was a smart and successful lawyer in New York City. He believed fervently in honesty and integrity, and lived his life aware of the fact that he could die tomorrow. When Jean was a college student visiting his family in France, he suddenly announced that he was going to ride a motorcycle to Pamplona to run with the bulls because, he told his friends and family, "everyone has to do something like that at least once in their life." According to Jean's brother, "He didn't want his epitaph to read, 'He went to law school; he went to Wall Street; he made a lot of money.'"

Jean was diagnosed with AIDS in the 1980s, when such a diagnosis was a death sentence. The drugs available at the time addressed the symptoms, but offered no hope for a cure. As Jean grew sicker, he refused to acknowledge his dying to those around him. He spoke instead of his plans for the future—a future everyone knew he would never have. He talked about going to the ocean for the summer, about the years that lay ahead, about cures. He never talked about his dying. But as everyone later learned, he thought about it quite a bit. Privately, with pen in hand, he had mapped out his dying and its aftermath. Among other things, he wrote a living will that included the following paragraph:

> I am committed to endure any treatment that can reasonably be expected to permit me to live a life in which I retain my personality and the ability to contribute in some way to the world around me. Don't keep me in a painful or vegetable state, or in a state with no reasonable hope of recovery to a productive lifestyle. I must be able to be more than a patient who is entirely dependent, in a sustained unconscious state, or devoid of the capacities for meaningful human interaction, thought, or feeling.

In this particular case it was just enough to guide his family through a crisis. Late in his illness, Jean developed an infection in his brain that left him deaf, almost blind, and increasingly uncommunicative. Oral antibiotics were not helping, and so it was suggested that he try intravenous antibiotics. Although this would not reverse the damage already done, it might keep him alive a little longer. His family didn't know what to do. Even his doctor was unsure of how to proceed. How aggressively should they try to keep him alive, given his condition?

"We were at this turning point," his sister-in-law recalled, "and I said, 'Let me read that paragraph again.' So I read it through and we all looked at each other and said, 'That means we do nothing more to stop this infection, right?' It was so clear. He said that if there is no hope of my returning to this level of functioning, please, that's when you should step back. It was a tremendous relief reading that paragraph because there was no doubt about what to do."

Jean didn't finish his final instructions there. He went on to provide his family with specific directions regarding his cremation and memorial service:

> I prefer that my remains be cremated and scattered to the winds. I hope I will live on in your hearts and in the warmth of your memories. What happens to my body is not important to me. . . . Should any memorial service be held, I urge that it reflect the Unitarian Universalist tradition. I believe in the search for truth. I request that any memorial be nondoctrinal; talk about all the life we shared rather than make tenuous predictions about whether I'll be in heaven or hell, or be reincarnated as a spirit. . . . I would also be offended by any suggestion that there must be some good or divine explanation for the timing or cause of my death.

His instructions were perfect; his strength and insight, astounding. If only we could all leave such a clear and loving message for our survivors.

death manners

ill at ease in the presence of death

Have you ever heard that a friend or acquaintance has a potentially
fatal disease and thought that you should send a note/call him/visit
her, but then, somehow, the note never gets written, the call never gets
made, the visit is always put off? Or have you been with someone who
is seriously ill, maybe run into him on the street or visited him in the
hospital, and suddenly found yourself feeling tense, unsure of what to
say or how to behave? If you are effusive, you might seem overly sym-
pathetic or depressing. On the other hand, if you are casual and light,
it might seem like you are denying what's happening or that you don't
care. If you are direct, well, what are you going to say? *I'm sorry about
your stage-three cancer. I hope you are feeling better soon.* It's a tough
situation and most of us don't handle it very well.

We can deal with a friend who has a broken leg or a bout of appendicitis, but when someone is terminally ill, most of us back away. Uncomfortable around death and afraid of doing something wrong, we find reasons not to do anything at all. Or we visit but we do so in protective groups and stand fidgeting by the doorway, or we steer the conversation to "safe" subjects—the weather, sports, neighborhood gossip. Maybe we flip on the television to avoid conversation, or we shield our discomfort with false words and empty hopes—"You're going to be fine."

We can learn all we want to about life support and advance directives, but if we can't be around people who are terminally ill, if we avoid them or get anxious when we are with them, all our learning will be for naught. We will not be able to have useful discussions about medical treatments, much less foray into conversations about life's meaning and its memorable moments. We will not be able to hear this person, be with him, console him in any way. We will not even be able to extend the most rudimentary acts of kindness—a neighborly visit, a kind note, a gentle word. Instead, we will silence people, isolate them, and intensify their pain.

I am guilty. I have detoured around visits, drafted words that were never put on paper and, sitting with someone who is ill, said all the wrong things. I have stumbled in the face of death, probably more times than I know. I recall one incident quite vividly, even though it happened nearly 15 years ago. It was one of those moments when time freezes, like when you're driving on a slippery road and the car begins to slide out of control, and seconds drag out like they are minutes, until the image of skidding into another car's back end is etched permanently into your mind. I had one of those moments with Edward Petraiuolo III.

Big Ed. We had gone to the same school for a few years, but he was a little older than me so I never really knew him—he was just a name and a face and a group of friends. Years later I saw Ed passing through the crowd at a football game. We recognized each other faintly, but rather than looking away, which is what I was about to do, Ed marched right over and introduced himself to me. He was like a big old friendly bear, treating me as if I were some dear friend, and before I knew it, he had convinced me to come down to the daily newspaper where he worked to meet some editors. A few days later, I found myself walking into the newsroom, unsure of how I had gotten myself into this, but in it nonetheless. An editor greeted me and informed me that Ed was sorry he couldn't be there to see me. He was in the hospital. Didn't I know that Ed had cancer, advanced cancer?

Ed couldn't have been much more than 28 at the time. And he was so, well, so alive. So fun-loving and outgoing and gregarious. He had so many friends and so much energy. How could he be so very sick?

I ended up working at the newspaper, but Ed and I saw little of each other because our beats didn't overlap, and because I'm not much of a partygoer, which Ed was. I remember a photo of Ed that was pinned to the bulletin board at work for some time. He was sitting at a bar, holding a frosty mug of beer, his friends all around him, and a wide grin on his face. That was Ed. Beer in hand, a circle of pals.

One day, less than a year into the job, I went to a meeting organized by some union representatives. The meeting was in the back of a crowded and dimly lit bar. People were jammed around tables, and standing two-deep along the walls. The union men had already begun their spiel when Ed walked in. No one else saw him; at least no one looked up. I hadn't seen him in months. He wore a long overcoat, which hung loosely around his now-thin frame. His head was bald and marked on one side with blue ink, indicating a radiation target. He slipped quietly into an empty seat by the door.

About an hour into the meeting I had to leave, and as I was walking out, zigzagging my way through the chairs, I realized that I was going to walk right past Ed. A wave of panic flowed through me. What would I say? What would I do? Before I could process any of this, Ed reached out and took my hand in both of his, looked me in the eye, and gave me a broad smile that embraced me, pulling me momentarily into the warm and optimistic world that was his. He was not nervous. He was not shy or reluctant or awkward. He was all Ed.

The greeting lasted for no more than a few seconds, but time stopped and I can still replay that tape today, all these dozen years later. I was startled by his ease and warmth, and I was ashamed that it was he who had reached out to me and offered me comfort, when I should have given that gift to him. I decided, as I was walking to my car, that the next time I saw him I would do a better job of this.

But I didn't get the chance. Two weeks later an editor announced to the newsroom that Ed had died that morning.

I hardly knew him, and yet, those words, ". . . Ed Petraiuolo died this morning . . . ," those solemn words, passed through my ears and poured like an icy fluid through my body. I sat before my computer terminal, stunned for a second, and then the tears rose up. I felt foolish crying in front of all these people who knew Ed so much better than I did, but I had no choice. I cried because Ed was too good to die, too young to die, too alive to die. And I cried because I had waited rather than reaching out. I hadn't shown him that I cared. I hadn't thanked him for his support. I hadn't opened myself to his kindness or friendship. And of course, now it was too late.

* * *

Obviously, there are far more consequential stories than this one—stories of people who postponed visiting a close friend or relative and then had only a funeral to attend; people who wanted desperately to say things, loving things, but could never find the words; people who wished they had asked about a person's life, a family's history, or a particular incident, but never got up the nerve; people who stayed away when they wanted to be near. One woman I know didn't visit her father when he was in the late stages of cancer because her visit "would have made it all seem too serious," and another almost didn't tell her father that she loved him for the same reason—as if her words of love would have made his dying too real.

Big or small, our failings hurt. They complicate our grief and prolong our pain. We are left with regrets that stay with us like festering wounds. We don't have the sense of closure or feelings of intimacy we so desire. Even small slips—a dismissive comment or postponed visit or, in my case, a failed greeting—hurt. They hurt because we want to help, we want to be a friend. We want to let someone know that we care. We want to make this journey—a journey we will take ourselves one day—easier. And when we don't know how to do that, we are left with only sorrow and regret.

The person who is ill is also hurt, of course. He may want to talk openly but is discouraged from doing so, may yearn for physical contact but is treated as if he were contagious, may need our friendship but sense our wariness. Being shut off by family members and loved ones hurts acutely, but even casual comments from neighbors, colleagues, and acquaintances can make a person feel abandoned, silenced, angry, and ashamed. It is this isolation and discomfort as much as anything else, sometimes as much as physical pain or medical intrusions, that makes dying today so difficult.

* * *

Carl Stevens felt the chill. Carl was at the leading edge of the baby boomers, and was representative of his generation in many ways. He was a good-looking man who had always been active and involved. He had a good education, worked in the financial world, married a wonderful woman, bought a comfortable home, and had two children—a daughter and a son. He spent his free time playing ice hockey and tennis, and enjoying his family and his friends. Shortly before he turned 50, Carl learned that he had amyotrophic lateral sclerosis—also known as Lou Gehrig's disease or motor neuron disease. ALS is an incurable illness in which a person's muscles become ineffectual, starting with the limbs and then moving to the lungs and throat, until the person cannot speak, swallow, or breathe. People with ALS typically die within five years of being diagnosed, although some live more than ten years, and a few as long as thirty.

Carl saw the awkwardness that comes with terminal illness. He knew that some people didn't visit him because they didn't know what to do or what to say, they didn't know what they would see or how they should respond. Those who did visit often became nervous. Early on, some refused to believe that Carl was as sick as he was. They urged him to "try harder." They said that if he worked at it, he could do more things for himself. They encouraged him to get out, to go to restaurants, to his son's soccer games, to parties. Some people refused to acknowledge that he was sick at all, as if by denying the disease, they would make it disappear. "I remember one incident when I took my son to a birthday party," Carl said. "People came up to me and said, 'You look great. You're doing fine.' They were convincing themselves and trying to convince me that nothing was really wrong."

Carl's experience is common. One woman who was dying of pancreatic cancer told me that people would constantly tell her that everything was going to be fine. Or worse, they tried to commiserate by talking about their own benign aches and pains, as if they understood how she felt. "It's strange," she said. "People either disappear from your life or they take all your control away. They're worried about their own emotions and their own feelings. They say, 'This is harder on me than it is on you.' If you think about that for a second, it's unbelievable."

In her book, *Seeing the Crab: A Memoir of Dying*, Christina Middlebrook tells the story of her losing battle with breast cancer—the process, her reactions, and her internal struggle as death neared. Throughout the book she is incensed by the way people speak to her, downplaying the severity of her illness, questioning her decisions about treatment, and encouraging her to be optimistic. At one point, after she had had several positive biopsies and was awaiting the results of yet another, a friend said to her, "My mother had a biopsy recently and it was negative. . . . So maybe yours will be good."

Christina's family couldn't seem to accept or understand—despite repeated explanations—that cancer had been detected in her spine and, having had this recurrence, a cure was no longer possible; she was fighting only for a little more time—months, possibly a year. Her mother told her at one point that she should focus her attention on the patients who had survived for several years, adding that such thoughts would help turn her into one of those patients. "These words *enrage* me," Christina writes. (The emphasis is hers.) "The mere assumption that good thoughts will affect the outcome of my life or death-revealing bone scans turns me ugly as Medusa. . . . 'Why didn't *thinking right* work in the beginning, when *none of us* thought that lump would turn out to be cancer?'" she yells at her mother.

Soon after that episode her brother says, "Maybe you'll have only *one* recurrence." Middlebrook is taken aback by the ignorance of the comment. "I sigh the deep sigh of the lonely," she says. "One recurrence is all it takes. I cannot breathe for the loneliness."

*　*　*

We have no intention of hurting anyone; we simply respond reflexively. The words come out of nowhere. *You will be fine. Don't talk that way. Think positive.* Like a protective hand rising up to block a slap, the words pop out to fend off a truth that stings. We blurt them out because, even though we know that one recurrence is one too many, we want to believe that things will be fine, that this disease will go away, that none of this is happening. *Everything is going to be fine.* We want it to be true, we want it so desperately, so intensely, that we try to force it to be true by insisting that it is. *Everything is going to be fine.* In the convoluted, illogical zone our brains inhabit at such a time, trying to wish away this nightmare, we believe that we must, at the very least, make sure the patient believes this is true. *Everything is going to be fine.* Of course, the patient isn't tricked by such simple words. The patient, in almost every case, knows exactly what is happening. The patient knows that everything will not be fine.

"There's a great deal of discomfort," says Barbara Guilfoyle, director of social work services at Calvary Hospital in the Bronx, which specializes in the care of terminally ill patients. "People often say, 'I don't know what to say. I know what's going on, but I don't want Mom to know.' Mom knows. And the family knows. But there's this great secrecy and a lot of energy goes into keeping the secret."

I have seen it myself, repeatedly. One incident occurred many years ago, long before I started this book. I was in a hospital room with a friend whose father was dying of metastatic brain cancer ("metastatic" means that cancer has spread to other parts of the body). My friend paced at the foot of his father's bed, looking out the window and then at me and then at the floor—anywhere but at his father—talking with animated energy about the fall weather, about the cheap hospital decor, about the new football season. All the while, his father was silent and tense. His eyes followed his son around the room and finally rested on an empty chair in the corner. He looked like a schoolboy trying to behave, trying not to cry, trying to be stoic. I sat beside him, holding his hand and mindlessly stroking his arm, saying nothing, not sure of my role. After some time, the father looked up at his son and whispered, "I'm frightened." I remember those words distinctly. They were so small, so quiet, and yet so enormous. They were an entryway into a world we had never, in all his months of illness, entered or even ventured near. They were a cue for us to share in and relieve his fears, to hold him, to be with him on a very human level, at an ever-so-human time. I met his pleading eyes and was about to ask him what, what was he afraid of, when his son blurted out, "Oh Dad, there's nothing to be afraid of. Everything's going to be all right." The subject never came up again. He died alone in that room with the cheap decor, full of fear, three days later.

Distanced from death, we have lost our social mores, our rituals, and any familiarity with death people once had. We have lost our customs and our manners, and no one is teaching them to us. No one tells us when to visit or what to say or how to behave. I searched through several books on etiquette to see if this subject was addressed, and what I found was pages upon pages on wedding protocol, entertaining, job applications, travel, and proper dress. There was advice on how to approach someone who has adopted a child, gotten divorced, or been fired from a job. There was even a fair amount of information on what to do after a death—how to deal with funerals, bereavement, condolences, flowers, and legacies. One book had a few pages on how to visit a sick friend and how to behave as a patient in the hospital. ("A woman should bring her prettiest bed jacket," says Amy Vanderbilt.) In the 2,100 pages on etiquette that I searched, I found five paragraphs—less than a page—on what to do when someone is terminally ill.

♣ Be there. Visit. Call. Write. Even if this is not someone you know well, push yourself to make the effort. As you confront your fears of death and learn more about the process of dying, it will become easier. But in the beginning, you will have to make a concerted effort to override the voice that says, "Maybe tomorrow."

A visit doesn't have to be long; in fact, even if you know the person well, visits should be short, as the patient is likely to be tired, and having guests is exhausting. Fifteen to twenty minutes is plenty of time. Don't stay and chat with the family either, for they, too, are weary. If the patient asks you to stay, use your good judgment; sometimes it is better to leave and promise that you will return soon. If you sense that this person truly wants your company, you might suggest that you will sit quietly and read a book or watch television with him. If you are visiting in a group, feel free to talk among yourselves, without forcing the person who is ill into the conversation. Very often, people just want to have others in the room, but they don't want to make an effort.

Flowers are often appreciated, but bring them or send them with a vase so no one has to fuss with cutting and finding containers. You might give a framed photo, perhaps of the two of you in happier times, or books on tape, or fruit. If you bring food, find out if the patient is on any special diet. Food is often a better gift for the family, who may be spending long days caring for this person, and may not have time for grocery shopping or cooking. A prepared dinner, preferably something that can be frozen if it is not needed immediately, is best. Sometimes the best visitors are the invisible ones, the people who drop off a hot meal at the family's home in the evening and leave without a word.

When visiting, don't expect the patient or family to act as hosts. Don't stand around waiting for someone to make conversation, or ask you to sit, or offer you something to eat. You are there to provide support, not to get it. In fact, before you leave, you should ask what you can do to help. Make some suggestions, like picking up groceries, getting books or videos from the library, making a meal, providing guest rooms for visiting relatives, or coming to visit during certain hours when others are not available.

As for letters, they too can be short. Let the person know that you heard about his illness and are thinking of him. There should be no suggestion that you expect a reply to your note. If you have the urge to say more, do so, but do it carefully. Don't take a funereal tone, talking as if the person were already dead—a eulogy, remembering milestones in his life. Let him know that his illness has made you think about him and all that he means to you. You might call or write a note to family members as well, letting them know that they are in your thoughts and prayers, and that you are eager to help in any way you can.

❧ **Be at ease.** Whatever you do, take a deep breath and try to be yourself. People who have a serious illness say that the one thing they want is normalcy. They want others to behave just as they always have, to laugh and gossip and talk as if nothing has changed. That doesn't mean avoiding the subject; it means being natural and allowing life to go on.

If someone is quite ill and looks that way, leave any disgust or fear at the door. If possible, get a description of how this person looks and what his capabilities are before you visit so you are not caught off guard and visibly shocked when you walk in. If you don't have a description, brace yourself for the fact that your friend may look very different. Give yourself a second to take in his appearance—that's to be expected—but get past it quickly. Don't focus attention on how thin or feeble or different he looks. (Although you certainly can ask about his health and spirits.) Keep firmly in your mind who he is and all that he means to you.

Your ease, and particularly your ability to see past the illness to the person, will be contagious and welcomed. It will put others at ease and will remind the person who is ill that, in your eyes and heart, he is still the person he always was.

Sit comfortably close and speak directly to him. Do not speak to others in the room as if this person were not present or able to hear. He might not be able to understand all you are saying, but he will certainly hear the tone of your voice, your concern and respect, your soothing familiarity and easy rhythm.

If you think you can't be at ease, if you think you won't be able to handle seeing this person in his new form, then you have to decide whether or not it's a good idea to visit. It's a personal decision, dependent upon the relationship, and whether you think your visit, however you respond, will be beneficial or detrimental to either or both of you.

♣ **What to say, how to listen.** If you don't know what to say, and most of us don't, say just that. "I don't know what to say," or "I can't imagine how you feel," or "Tell me what I can do to help," or "What is going on with you?" And then listen. Really listen.

Let the patient guide the conversation. Ask open-ended questions, see where he wants to go, and then go there with him. Don't shut a person off with comments like, "You'll be fine," or "Don't be down." Instead, ask why he thinks he won't be fine and what worries him, or how you might help him feel less depressed.

While you shouldn't try to steer the conversation to safe subjects, you also don't want to force a "heavy" discussion. If the patient wants to talk about his illness, let him. If he wants to discuss his fears, allow it. If he wants to talk about the weather or politics or finances or neighborhood gossip, that's fine too. Ill people often want to hear the normal, the routine, the usual. They want to hear something funny or happy or ridiculous. There is nothing wrong with talking about everyday things as long as that's what the patient wants to do.

A person's cues can be subtle and openings can come up unexpectedly, which is why you need to listen carefully. Someone might suddenly say something like, "I'm going to miss you," or "I want to get you a birthday present early this year," or "I need to talk with a lawyer." You don't want to be caught off guard and respond defensively, so be ready. The patient may be feeling you out, to see if you are going to allow this kind of conversation to occur. Let him know that you will. Open the way for him to explain the comment, to take it further if he wants to. For example, if he says that things look bleak, ask him how so. If he says a test result was bad, ask him what it means and what is going to happen next. If he says he is angry, ask him why.

Late in an illness, when the patient's mind is less clear, his comments may be even less direct. He might mention a friend or relative who died years ago or talk about going on a trip—getting tickets, packing bags, that sort of thing. Instead of saying, "You don't need a suitcase. You're not going anywhere," you might say, "Where are you going? Is it a nice place?" Or you might say, "I know you have to go and I will miss you."

Whatever you talk about, be sure that you don't treat this person like a child. Don't dismiss his comments, negate his feelings, or take away his control. Remember, this is an adult going through an extremely adult experience. (Or it may be a child going through an extremely adult experience, which requires equally respectful responses.) If a person wants to smoke, pray, yell, cry, lay blame, worry, or skip their pain medications, he has a right to do that. Rather than telling him to calm down, you might say, "I don't blame you for being angry," and then hand him a pillow to punch or let him vent at you for a while. If he says he is worried about his family's finances or how someone he loves will get on, rather than saying, "Oh, don't worry about that," let him talk about these worries in real terms and treat his concerns seriously—because they are serious.

If you ever feel that you've said the wrong thing, cut someone off, or dismissed some concern—which we are all certain to do—that's okay. Don't be hard on yourself. This is an extremely difficult time, and allowing blunt conversations about unfathomable issues calls for unnatural strength. You might simply brace yourself to be more open the next time around, or try to revisit the conversation. "Dad, the other day you said you are going to miss me. I just want you to know that I heard you, I love you, and I am going to miss you too."

the next generation

teaching our children about death

We have an opportunity not only to improve our own lot, but to make sure that the next generation is better able to cope with death and dying when they come upon it. And so, as we learn about death ourselves, we also need to teach our children about mortality, the dying process, the rituals of death, and the ensuing grief. To do this, we must talk honestly with them, listen to their thoughts and questions, and support them through any personal loss.

Most of us instinctively shield our children from pain and sorrow. With good intentions, we guide them to things that are joyful and easy, and keep them from things that are upsetting. When we visit a seriously ill relative in the hospital, we leave the children at home; when we go to a funeral, we send the children to a friend's house; and when we talk about death, we keep our voices hushed. This, we decide, is "too much" for them, "it doesn't involve them," they're "too young to understand."

But children, even very young children, know when something is askew. They hear what is said, especially when it is said in low, serious voices. They are aware of the disruption of the household. They feel the distress of their parents and others. And they are deeply affected by it. When we don't explain what is happening, we leave them to imagine the worst and to cope with their feelings alone. And we leave them with the message that this subject is taboo.

In one of my earliest memories I am about four years old, standing on the blacktop of our driveway. The hedge of yellow forsythia is in full bloom. I am being shuffled over to a station wagon as my best friend's mother explains to me that I am going to their house for the night because my grandmother has died and my parents are going to the funeral. Died? I was bewildered. What was that about? Why hadn't my parents told me about this? And why had I been left behind?

Children have varying abilities to comprehend death. Child psychologists and grief experts say that children become vaguely aware of death as young as two or three. They know that things die, and certainly, if a death occurs close to home, they will be keenly aware that something serious has happened and that people in the household are upset. At this age, you can begin to introduce the concept of death to a child by talking about the squirrel that is killed on the road, the leaves that fall from a tree, cut flowers that begin to droop.

By age five, children understand that people die, but they tend to see it as a temporary state and cannot—no matter how much you explain it—understand that someone can be gone forever. Theirs is a sort of Wile E. Coyote view of death. The cartoon coyote, in his endless quest for the roadrunner, drops off the edge of canyons and gets clobbered by anvils, but he is always back to the drawing board in the next scene.

Between the ages of five and nine, children begin to realize that death is irreversible, yet they tend to think that it can't happen to them or anyone in their family. They may also view death as being some sort of boogeyman who comes and takes people away. From nine to twelve, they understand the permanence of death and that it is a biological process. They might feel threatened by death, and some become interested in skeletons, ghosts, coffins, and other death images. Dr. Elisabeth Kübler-Ross, in *On Death and Dying,* says that children will sometimes feel guilt-ridden, believing that they are in some way responsible for the death of a parent or other loved one. Because they can't differentiate between a wish and a deed, she explains, they may recall some moment when they wished a parent would die or disappear, and reason that this is simply a wish coming true. Others may feel, as in a divorce, that because they were bad or unlovable, they caused the disappearance of their relative or friend.

Finally, during their teen years, most children realize that they themselves could die. As a defense, or maybe in defiance, they sometimes act as if they don't care. They might decide that they are immortal and engage in reckless, dangerous behaviors. Teens will respond to the death of someone they love much as an adult would. The loss of a parent during these turbulent years can be unbearable.

when children are about

⚜ **Be open about death.** When my son Jack was three or four, I took a stack of books out of the library one day without reading through them. One book appeared to be about a boy's love for his grandmother, but as I began reading it to him that night I realized that while it was about that love, it was also about the subsequent death of Grandma, and the boy's grief over that loss. As soon as I realized where the story was heading, I said something like, "Oh, this is sad. Let's read a different book," and laid it down by the bedside. But my son's interest was piqued. Not only did he demand that we finish it, but over the next few days it was the first book he grabbed each time we sat down to read. At first, I hid the book under the stack, hoping he would forget about it. But he didn't, and finally I gave in. I read it. Over and over. He asked a trail of questions, and I struggled to answer them. ("Mommy, will you and Daddy die one day?" "Do I have to die?" "If everyone dies, does that mean that one day there won't be any people left on the Earth?") It was awkward for me. I didn't like having this conversation with my little boy. I wanted to talk about something else. Anything else. But gradually I realized that this conversation wasn't frightening to him. It wasn't scaring him. He was simply curious, and this was an opportunity for us to discuss death matter-of-factly, when we were not dealing with a real death.

A year later, when Jack's paternal grandmother was terminally ill, I was glad that we had had those discussions, because now we could fall back on them. He was clear and direct about it all, but also very tender. He visited his grandmother at her home, where she was under the care of a hospice program. He played in her wheelchair, brought her flowers, and then, when she died, drew a touching picture of her with hearts all around, which he placed on her coffin. I was proud of him, and also grateful that he had pushed me into a conversation that I was reluctant to have.

It's not necessary to run out and buy children's books about death (although there are good ones available, some of which are listed at the end of this chapter), nor is it necessary to force a discussion about death. But when the subject comes up—certainly if there is a death in the family, but even if there is a death in a movie, a death in the community, or the death of a pet—fight the urge to insulate your children. Encourage their questions and be open and honest with your answers.

You can be selective in the information you provide, and you should certainly explain anything in terms that are appropriate for the age of the child. There's no point in discussing the pros and cons of specific medical treatments or the details of some agonizing symptom with a five-year-old. But you can explain that a grandparent is seriously ill and is not expected to live long.

⚜ Initiate the conversation. When a family friend or relative is terminally ill, children often don't ask questions because they are not sure if this is safe turf, or because they simply don't know what questions to ask. They only know that something unusual is going on and they are scared by it. Instead of asking questions, they might adopt your stress and turn into whining tyrants, further straining your meager emotional reserve. Rather than helping them to cope with death, you find yourself screaming at them to leave you alone.

It may be up to you to start the conversation. Explain what is going on, and why you are upset. Ask your children if they have any questions. Let them know that you are there for them if there is anything they want to talk about. And then raise the subject again later.

Adolescents, in particular, may be reluctant to open up. They might act detached, as if they don't care. Work within their framework. Don't force them to express their feelings, but let them know that you are available. They might talk more freely if you discuss your own fears, sadness, and confusion, if you admit that you feel empty or angry. Or you might discuss your feelings with someone else, within earshot of the youth. That often gives them permission to explore their own stew of conflicted emotions.

No matter the age of the child, encourage discussion long after the loved one has died. Dealing with death is a process that never ends. Children will have questions and concerns for years after Grandpa or Mom or Aunt Grace has died.

♣ Be ready when they are. Unfortunately, children don't always talk on your schedule, when you are off the phone, ready and available. More often, they want to talk when you can't. And they don't "save" their questions and emotions for later. So when you ask, "Honey, what's up?" they insist it was "nothing."

Do whatever you can to be available on their schedule. Put down the phone, stop cooking, turn off the television. Let them know that their questions and reactions are important and worthy of your full attention.

♣ Avoid euphemisms. Children, as well as adults, do better with honest explanations. If you say that Granny has gone to sleep and will never wake up, or that God has taken her, or that she has gone on a long trip and will never come back, you may find that your child doesn't want to go to bed, take a trip, or have much to do with God.

Dr. Paul Brinich, clinical professor of psychology and psychiatry at the University of North Carolina, tells the story of a young child, two or three years old, who had a fit when her father was at the airport about to leave on a business trip. She didn't want her father to fly and insisted that he not leave. It turned out that her grandmother had died recently and the parents had explained that Grandma had gone to heaven, which was up in the sky. Now here was Dad about to get on a plane and go up into the sky. She put two and two together and was not letting anyone she cared about leave the ground.

Of course the parents may not have been speaking euphemistically; they may have been relaying what they perceived to be the truth. But a young child takes these messages more literally than we imagine. So we need to think things through before we offer such explanations.

Be honest, even if that means saying that you don't know the answer to some questions. And don't push the conversation beyond the child's interest or level of understanding. Keep it simple and then let them push the conversation as far as they want it to go.

🌿 **Listen carefully.** More important than what you say is what you hear. When you talk about death, explain the situation and then listen. Ask young children to explain their understanding of what you've said. Often what seems like a clear explanation to our ears is completely misconstrued by a youngster.

Also, children are often concerned about issues that wouldn't occur to a grown-up. They might have practical concerns (*Who's going to live in Grandma's room now?*), they might have scientific questions (*Won't she be cold in the ground? Can she see me still?*), or they might be haunted by frightening thoughts (*Will anyone else in our family die too? Is this illness contagious?*). The only way you'll know what is on their minds is to ask and listen.

🌿 **Let them take part.** When there is a death or illness in the family's inner circle, be aware of a child's involvement and needs. Our habit of ignoring children at these times is a bad one. Children have much to gain from these experiences, for not only do they learn that death is a natural event, but they also need this involvement just as adults do, to help them grieve.

When someone is sick, let children help if they want to. A young child might comb Grandma's hair, help assemble her dinner, or entertain her. Children can be quite compassionate and often want very much to help; they simply don't know how.

The big question is, should you bring children to funerals or to visit loved ones who are near death? In general, the answer is yes. Although we worry that children will be upset, they are often more frightened by what they don't see than by what they do. Furthermore, they need the chance to say good-bye. However, there may be cases when a visit is not advisable. For example, when a patient is so disfigured and unrecognizable the visit will only be upsetting for the child. Use your own judgment—and, to some extent, the child's judgment. Explain what the visit will be like, and then let the child decide if he or she wants to come. Children as young as five or six can often make such a decision for themselves.

If you bring children along, don't expect them to be solemn or quiet or even particularly well behaved. It's hard not to snap at them because, of course, your nerves are already sizzling like a severed electrical wire. But try to remember that children are not being disrespectful; they are being children. They may be bored; they may be responding to the stress of others; or they might be trying to cope with their own grief. Like adults, children can only tolerate so much. Keep visits brief. If you bring children to a funeral, especially a lengthy one, bring some small treats and quiet activities along, and try to have someone on hand who can accompany them if they want to leave.

As for whether a dying person should come home to die when there are children in the house, Dr. Kübler-Ross addresses that question beautifully in her book *To Live Until We Say Good-bye*. "Children are overjoyed to have a parent out of the hospital and back at home," she says. Whatever restrictions are placed on them—to be quiet or not have friends over—were outweighed by having a parent near. "The most important thing, no matter how ill a parent is, is for a child to be near his or her mother or father, to have them physically close and not isolated and away at a hospital where children can never visit," she says.

♣ **Create memorials.** Children should be encouraged to do something to memorialize a loved one who has died, to recognize the relationship and the loss. Young children might draw pictures or make flowers to put with the coffin or in a special place in the house. Older ones might create a scrapbook, organize photos, or write poetry or a story about the relationship. All of this helps them to grieve and accept death and, perhaps, face it a little more openly and less fearfully in the future.

A number of books can help children understand death. Here are a few good ones:

For preschool children:
> *The Dead Bird* by Margaret Wise Brown, illustrated by Remy Charlip. (Young Scott Books)
> *The Tenth Good Thing About Barney* by Judith Viorst, illustrated by Erik Blegvad. (Atheneum)

For children 5 to 8:
> *Annie and the Old One* by Miska Miles, illustrated by Peter Parnall. (Little Brown & Co.)

Nana Upstairs and Nana Downstairs by Tomie DePaola. (Putnam)

My Grandpa Died Today by Joan Fassler. (Human Sciences Press)

The Fall of Freddie the Leaf by Leo F. Buscaglia. (Holt Rinehart Winston)

For children 8 and up:

A Taste of Blackberries by Doris B. Smith. (Thomas Y. Crowell Co.)

Charlotte's Web by E. B. White, illustrated by Garth Williams. (HarperCollins)

The Birds' Christmas Carol by Kate Douglas Wiggin. (Houghton-Mifflin)

III
avoiding common obstacles

the spiral of hope

when hope is not helpful

The next four chapters look at attitudes people often adopt in the face of death which, while not wrong, and in fact quite natural, often make death and the decisions that surround it more difficult. By simply being aware of these behaviors we can watch for them in ourselves and, perhaps, keep them in check. The first of these is hope.

For centuries, doctors and patients alike took the Cartesian view that the body was simply a cluster of parts working independently of the mind. The mind, and all that came with it—stress, fear, hope, anger, sadness—was thought to have no effect on the machinery of the body. Emotional responses were seen as nothing more than annoyances, something a doctor could ignore and a patient had to bear.

But our thinking on all this has changed. In the past few decades, it has become increasingly evident that the mind is affected by the body, and the body is influenced, sometimes deeply, by the mind. Researchers have discovered that illness and chronic pain can trigger or worsen depression and anxiety, and that oppressive emotions can contribute to disease. Most of us don't need scientific studies to tell us this. We know it from personal experience. We are more apt to get colds when we are exhausted, asthma attacks when we are stressed, and cold sores when we are anxious.

More recently, doctors and other observers have taken this a step further and suggested that not only do "bad" emotions affect our health, but "good" ones seem to have an impact as well. Through books such as Norman Cousins's *Anatomy of an Illness*, Bernie Siegel's *Love, Medicine and Miracles*, and Bill Moyers's *Healing and the Mind*, we have learned that positive emotions can actually be healing. Love, friendship, optimism, and a strong spirit apparently help us battle disease and stay healthy.

In addition to a patient's general frame of mind, his belief in the power of a particular treatment also seems to have a measurable effect. Doctors have known for some time that patients who think that they are receiving an effective treatment, even when they are not, often show signs of improvement, or at least get worse more slowly—something called the "placebo effect"—a placebo being a dummy pill or treatment. Researchers claim that patients receiving nothing but fake treatments have actually grown hair, avoided allergic reactions, recovered from depression, and escaped asthma attacks. Similarly, patients who falsely believed that they were exposed to allergens or infections actually developed rashes, nausea, pain, and other symptoms, even though actual exposure never occurred.

Given all this talk about the power of the mind and, particularly, the power of positive thinking, it may seem odd that something as fortifying as hope could contribute to a bad death. The fact is, hope is good; it is vital to any patient, or to any person, for that matter. But when we stubbornly and rigidly cling to hope that is unrealistic, it is no longer hope, but desperation, and this can have devastating effects, both on the patient's mood and on his course of treatment. As you will see, in the voyage from the first office visit to the bedside of a terminally ill patient, the distortion of hope is understandable, and almost inevitable unless we have a very good guide or some real understanding of the nature and benefits of hope. The scene painted here also shows, as an important aside, that quite often the way we die is not the fault of one doctor or one family member or one bad call; it is the result of a series of subtle comments and misunderstandings.

A doctor, test results in hand, stands in his office feeling uneasy. He (or she) is just about to relay some very bad news and does not want to devastate the patient. When the patient comes in and sits down, the doctor looks for some way to soften the blow and to give this poor person some hope. He explains the test results and the diagnosis and perhaps mentions that this is a serious situation, but then, sensing the patient's anguish, he moves on quickly to discuss treatment options and possibilities. He mentions a particular treatment that has helped some patients, or an experimental therapy that has unknown benefits. He presents statistics, but focuses on the positive—the patients who have survived or done better than the others. For example, rather than saying that most people with this disease die within a year, he points out that some patients have survived for many years. Perhaps he uses expressions like "effective treatment" and "remission" and "promising intervention," and cushions his words with phrases like "it seems" or "it is uncertain" or "let's see what further tests show." The doctor is not trying to mislead the patient in any way; he is simply trying to make this as easy as possible and to give the patient hope. And the truth is, at this point, there may be room for this sort of hope.

Doctors are criticized for not being more honest with their patients, but the truth is that they simply don't know what the future holds. And even if they have a good guess, it's hard news to deliver. Imagine yourself in the doctor's place, telling someone you hardly know, or worse, someone you know very well, that they have a potentially fatal disease.

Dr. Elizabetth Beautyman, an internist at Roosevelt Hospital in New York, who often deals with leukemia patients, says that it's a grim task. "When you're first telling someone that they have leukemia, they've gone from a completely happy, normal, worry-free existence to being told they have something which they know in the back of their mind is terminal," she says. "You have to give them some hope. You have to emphasize the positive so they can cope with all they need to cope with in the days ahead.

"It's a horrible illness to have and the treatment is difficult," Dr. Beautyman says. When she first relates the diagnosis, patients sometimes fall apart, sobbing in her office, so she struggles to give them something positive, some bit of hope, they can hang on to. "I tell patients that there is a 70 percent chance of them going into complete remission," she said. Seventy percent sounds promising. But then she explains: "Of course, complete remission doesn't mean cure. There's a lot of relapse that happens and without further treatment, in two years they will be sick again.

"It's very hard to deliver bad news," she adds, "and the messenger often doesn't get it right no matter what they do."

Meanwhile, no matter what dreadful diagnosis has been handed down, the patient in our scenario is in complete shock. The doctor is talking, but his words are lost in a swelling sea of sadness and disbelief. This cannot be happening. It cannot be true. It is not possible. There must be a way out of it. The doctor's words drone on, but the patient hears only snippets of what is being said. He is trying to stay afloat, to regain some balance. He is picturing his wife, his children, his future. His mind drifts through the facts and possibilities that are being presented, ignoring that which it can't yet fathom, and grabbing hold of anything that might make this nightmare more bearable.

Of course, the patient will find more hope if that is what the doctor is offering, if that is how the information is presented. But even if the doctor doesn't sugarcoat the news, even if she is excruciatingly blunt about the situation, a patient will often block out what he can't bear to hear, insist that the doctor is wrong, or find some statistic or theory or case that suggests a cure.

"Patients don't listen because they don't want to hear bad news. That's clearly the truth," says Dr. David Weissman, an oncologist who directs the palliative care program at the Medical College of Wisconsin in Milwaukee. "There are a zillion studies showing that patients don't hear anything you tell them even when you're blunt." In his days as a full-time oncologist, Dr. Weissman says he often found himself talking to people about chemotherapy that he knew was a waste of time, but "they really wanted it because they were looking for hope."

Who wouldn't respond in such a way? Dr. Kübler-Ross says that denial is not only a natural response at this point in an illness, but a necessary one—one that doctors should expect. The psyche is incapable of digesting so much bad news at one moment, so the patient looks for an out, hears information selectively, and directs all of his questions toward hope—the chance that the diagnosis is wrong, the opportunities for surgery, the probability that a certain medication will help, the new study that just came out, the patients who have survived.

In any case, the doctor in our scenario feels that he has presented the situation clearly, but as time passes, he sees that the patient remains focused on the slim odds of survival and on treatment options. The patient isn't asking about palliative care. He isn't acknowledging any possibility of death. He is interested only in finding a treatment. Quite honestly, the doctor is accustomed to this route and he is glad that the patient has hope. Who knows, even under dire circumstances this patient might do better than others, and having hope, as far as the doctor is concerned, is vitally important. Throughout their training and careers, doctors are taught—if not explicitly, then implicitly— that they must maintain a patient's hope, even if they know that such hope is unrealistic.

"There's a widespread belief among doctors that hope is the most important thing and that there's no real cost to allowing patients to have somewhat unrealistic expectations about their prognosis," says Dr. Jane Weeks, director of the Center for Outcomes and Policy Research at the Dana-Farber Cancer Institute in Boston. "We all want to leave a patient with some hope. It's a nice thing to give a patient. The question is, is there a cost to that?"

As we will see, there is a cost, but for the moment let's return to our scenario. The doctor and patient have established a rapport, but family members are also in the picture. Somewhere along the course of this illness they realize, on some level, that the illness is terminal, or possibly terminal, and maybe they even mention this out of the patient's earshot. Yet, at the same time, they can't fathom that this person—a person whom they love dearly, a person who is a fixed part of their lives—could actually die. It can't be. It's not possible.

Feeling helpless and distressed, they turn to the doctor for reassurance. "What can be done?" they ask. "What sorts of treatments are available?" They wait expectantly. The doctor may be more up-front with the family than he is with the patient, but he wants to be kind and he senses their need to take action, so once again, he couches his words in hope. He tells the family that the patient seems to be doing well, that he is strong, that this or that treatment might help, that some patients survive for many years. Family members, like the patient, embrace any sliver of optimism. They, too, hear selectively and focus on what might be. They are determined to help their loved one. They will get the best care possible for him. They will fight to keep him alive. And they will make sure that he has hope.

They don't talk about "end-of-life" care; they talk about "prolonging-life" care. They talk about the next test, the next treatment, the good signs. They talk about getting stronger or better. They talk about the future. They don't discuss the possibility of death because it is too painful, because they want to maintain hope, and because they don't want to believe that death is a possibility. They are so focused on keeping the patient hopeful that, in many cases, they not only stress the positives, they hide the negatives.

Sharon Tompkins remembers clearly the day she discovered, out of the blue, that her first husband, Aram, had incurable brain cancer. The couple were standing on the rocky steps of a canal in Key West, Florida, pulling on their snorkeling fins, when Aram, who was 53 at the time, suddenly made a strange face and his head began to twitch. At first Sharon thought her husband was clowning around, but then she realized that he was not grimacing on purpose and that, furthermore, he could not speak. After many stressful hours, Sharon stood in a doctor's office at the Miami Heart Institute staring at a blotchy gray scan of her husband's brain.

The doctor pointed to a small, white blur and explained that Aram had "the most serious kind of tumor and it doesn't respond to treatment." The average life span for someone in his situation was two months to two years. Sharon could barely breathe.

She gathered herself and walked into the hallway, where her husband sat waiting in a wheelchair. She looked at him, tried to clear her face of anguish, and told him that the doctors had found "a growth."

"I didn't tell him that this was the worst kind of tumor that didn't respond to treatment," she said. "I didn't feel that was something that he really needed to know because, why take away hope? I said to him, 'We don't know what it is, it could be malignant, it could be benign, but there's a growth.'" In the eleven months of her husband's illness until his death (which actually took place at home and was loving and tender), Sharon doesn't remember ever telling him his prognosis.

We hide or dilute the facts—or refuse to learn them in the first place—to protect ourselves and to protect the patient. We do it because at this moment we love this person more than anything in the world. We do it because we can't face what is happening and we certainly don't want the patient to have to face it.

The problem is that people have the right to information about their own health. They need to know what's happening so that they can make decisions about how they will proceed. And they need the option of discussing the truth with their loved ones so that they can pursue any goals they might have, and begin to accept what is happening.

The irony is, the patient does know. In virtually every case, no matter what is said or unsaid, the patient knows the truth—in fact, knows it better than anyone else.

"Time after time patients recount to doctors, including me, how they have known almost since they first went to their doctor but kept up the pretense of ignorance, not so much for their own sake but for the sake of others, particularly the family—but also for the doctor," Dr. Doyle says in *Caring for a Dying Relative.*

The patient often agrees to more treatments and consults and tests because he is too exhausted to fight, too sick to care, and too afraid to upset anyone more than he already has. Being the "good" patient, he goes along with whatever is suggested and adopts whatever attitude is expected of him. His family, the doctor, the nurses, and other health care professionals admire him for his "fighting spirit." They like that he is hopeful, and so, that is what he will be. They want him to continue treatment, and so that is what he will do.

"I can't tell you how many people get chemotherapy not because they want it, but because they think their family wants them to get it," Dr. Weissman says. "We had a young girl, 24, recently on our unit. Bad cancer. Clearly dying. The family wanted her to get another round of chemotherapy. The personal physician wasn't coming to see her. The doctors who were taking care of her in the hospital weren't sure what to do. I was asked to see her solely for pain. I walked in and she looked terrible. I said, 'What are you thinking about?' and she said, 'I want to go home.' She'd been in the hospital for about three weeks at this point. I said, 'You know what that means?' She said 'Yes.' I said, 'You're dying.' She said, 'Yes, I know. I want to go home. That's what I want right now.' We talked about that and I said, 'How do your parents feel about that?' She said something to the effect of, 'They'll get over it.' She said they'd have a hard time. She said, 'I'm tired. I don't want any more tests. I don't want any more needles. I don't want any more.'

"You have to give them permission sometimes," Dr. Weissman says. "You have to either say it for them or give them permission to say it. It's never a surprise to people that they are dying. They always know. But they've not been able to verbalize it. They've been waiting for some doctor to tell them, so they really know. Many people will say, 'Gee, I thought so.'"

Unfortunately, in most cases, no one opens the door to such straightforward conversation. They don't offer the information or consider the fact that the patient might like to have such information. They don't discuss the patient's prognosis, his needs, the goals of treatment, or the possibility of hospice or other palliative care. They don't venture into such taboo terrain because it is too painful, because they don't want to upset each other, and because they want to maintain hope.

Clearly, hope has enormous value and patients should absolutely be encouraged to be hopeful. The problem is not that people have hope; the problem is that they don't always differentiate between false and realistic hope. All too often what they consider to be hope is actually deception.

In the early stages of an illness, when there is much information and emotion to digest, denial and unrealistic optimism are not bad. But too often that optimism becomes a pattern, an obsession and, finally, a lie. The lie is planted without malice, but once it is established, no one dares uproot it. The patient is not healed by this lie, this forced hope. He is not uplifted or bolstered by it. Instead, he is isolated. Silenced. Shut off. Forced into complacency. He is left with no one with whom he can speak honestly, he is forced to be "optimistic," he is left feeling as if he were somehow to blame for this disease—*If only he were more positive he would get well*—and he is left getting medical treatments that are not necessarily what he wanted.

Dr. Weeks and her colleagues followed 917 terminally ill cancer patients and found that, indeed, hope does have a cost, not only in terms of emotional isolation, but in terms of the medical decisions that are made. According to the report, most patients in the study had unrealistic beliefs about their odds of survival and, based on those beliefs, opted for aggressive treatments. In other words, patients believed that their illness was not as serious as it was and that the treatments held more promise than they did.

"Patients didn't have a good understanding of their prognosis, which is information that they needed to make choices that were right for them," Dr. Weeks says. The study did not examine why patients had such unwarranted optimism, but Dr. Weeks suggests that it was due to a combination of factors—doctors offering undue optimism, and patients choosing to believe what they wanted.

As we've seen, this dance is complex. Each person takes his cues from the others, but he takes those cues selectively because he is unsure of how to proceed, reluctant to acknowledge the prospect of death, and trying as best as he can to sustain this magical thing called hope.

the changing nature of hope

First of all, let's be clear about what hope can and cannot do. Hope cannot cure terminal cancer or emphysema or a life-threatening blockage. Hope cannot shrink an aggressive tumor or eradicate a life-threatening infection. What hope can do is possibly give the immune system a little extra oomph, so that the body can put up a better fight. Even more vital than that, however, hope helps a person cope with a terrible situation. It helps him to live as fully as he can, to tend to important matters, to see value in life, and to rise to face each day.

The presence of hope is what distinguishes sadness, which is perfectly normal, from depression, which is paralyzing.

But in order for hope to have any benefit at all, it has to be based in reality. It has to be honest. We tend to operate within an extremely narrow definition of hope—the hope of beating death. But a person can have strong and fulfilling hope for all sorts of things. She might hope to finish a project, to see a grandchild born, or to make amends with a friend. Just because a person accepts that she will die does not mean that she is without hope.

A person can hope for all sorts of things and what she hopes for will probably change with time. In the early stages of a disease, a patient might hope for a cure. When that doesn't seem probable, she might hope to retain certain abilities, such as walking or living independently, for as long as possible. As the disease progresses further, she might hope to live until a certain date, such as an anniversary or a special holiday. As she grows more ill, she might hope that she will be free of pain and distressing symptoms, or that her loved ones will stay with her until the end. A dying patient may hope that her life has had meaning or that she will be remembered kindly or that she will gain closer unity with God.

Given the chance, people will adjust their goals, but not neatly along a continuum, like the one described above. Death and grief experts say that people go through stages when they are dying or grieving a death, starting with denial (*This can't be happening*), moving through anger (*Why me?*), bargaining (*God, I'll be really good if you let me get better*), and depression, until, if they are lucky, they reach acceptance. But they don't slide along, moving neatly from one response to the next in line. They go from one reaction to the other and back to a previous one—accepting, then angry, then bargaining, then depressed, then denying, and then accepting again.

The human mind is masterful at juggling a variety of beliefs and hopes at once, even seemingly contradictory ones. In some part of the brain people know that death is inevitable; in another part, they know that death is not possible. So when they talk of a cure or a long future, they are not lying to themselves or others; they are simply tuning into this other channel, this more pleasant and perhaps wistful part of the mind. It's a little like talking about winning the lottery. The possibility is remote, but it feels good to think about. It's a nice place to be. The trouble comes when the person says, "I'm going to win the jackpot," and others nod eagerly and say, "Oh yes, we are absolutely sure that you will." Or worse, he says that he probably won't win and they say, "Don't talk like that." They have not bolstered his hope of winning; they have created a credibility gap. *My word*, he thinks, *they really believe this*. Now it is on his shoulders not to let them down, and not to stray from this dream of "winning." If instead friends responded to his hopeful thinking by saying, "That would be great," and were open to his more honest moments, saying something like, "Does that scare you?" or simply, "Do you think so?" they would have allowed him to be wherever he needed to be, wistful or practical, without closing the door to other discussions.

We, the loved ones and others involved in a patient's care, need to find a way to embrace hope without creating deception. We need to allow dreaming without shutting off reality. We need to allow fear without becoming hopeless. We admire the "winning attitude," the patient who keeps up "the fight," but we also need to realize that just because a person accepts the severity of an illness does not mean she has lost hope or "given up." She has simply shifted her energies so that now, rather than fighting a disease, she may be fighting pain, isolation, and fear, or she may be working toward resolution, completion, or peace at the end of life.

Finally, although we tend to focus on hope, we need to remember that it is only one component of a "positive attitude." And when it comes to dying, it may not be the most important one. Yes, hope (real hope) is a good thing to have. But just as important, and integrally connected, are intimacy, honesty, spirituality, and joy of life. Just as people need hope, they also need to feel that they can be open, that they have the support of those they love, and that they are not alone.

As family members and friends, we need to have hope and to encourage hope, but we also need to be honest with the patient. We need to listen to him, recognize where he is and where his hopes lie, and be supportive of his goals, whatever they are and however they may fluctuate. We need to maintain his hope not by establishing unrealistic expectations but by valuing life and assuring him that we are with him and will continue to be with him, wherever this journey might lead.

carol's story

Carol Tatkon, a senior vice president at Exxon, was a mover and shaker in life. She was a brilliant woman who dealt with issues promptly, swiftly, and matter-of-factly. After a dinner party she'd go into the kitchen, assess the mess, set a timer for 12 minutes and say to her sister, "If it takes more than 12 minutes to clean this up, it's taking too long."

At 55, Carol was diagnosed with bladder cancer. She sought out medical care from oncologists at M.D. Anderson Cancer Center in Houston, Texas, one of the most renowned cancer centers in the world. Surgeons removed her bladder and she received chemotherapy for six months. She was fine after that—for 15 months. In August of 1995 the cancer reemerged in other parts of her body. She had more chemotherapy and then, the following March, she underwent aggressive surgery. As she explained it, doctors cut her open "from the chest all the way to the crotch" so they could "scoop out" whatever cancer they found. She was thrilled with the idea; her doctors told her that this could rid her of the disease completely. However, when the surgeon opened her up, he found so much cancer throughout her body that he simply stitched her back up without "scooping out" anything at all.

As Carol lay recuperating, the surgeon told her family that she had perhaps six months to live. When the news was later relayed to Carol, she was deeply saddened, but seemingly accepting of it. However, a couple of days later she saw her oncologist, who was undaunted by the results of the surgery and ignored the surgeon's prognosis. Carol's sister, Cathy Clark, says that he was extremely optimistic and determined to "make Carol better, to cure her."

Despite the surgeon's comments only days earlier, Carol didn't question the oncologist's optimism. In fact, she embraced it. She went on to try more chemotherapy, a new cancer drug that had just come on the market, and then more surgery to remove "tumors the size of tennis balls," as she put it, from her upper leg.

By December the news was very bad. Carol told me that she wasn't a good candidate for surgery or radiation because the cancer was so widespread, and that she had already received the highest dose of chemo available without success. "They're saying it's a very pervasive, persistent, resistant cancer," she said. Despite all this, she did not acknowledge that it was fatal or that nothing more could be done to fight the disease. "We're in a period where we're trying to gather research," she said.

I asked Carol how her 28-year-old daughter, Heather, was coping with this. "She kind of plays off me," she said, "and I tell her that I'm going to get well."

Six months later, Carol was still hoping for a cure when her oncologist suggested that she contact a local hospice. But, according to Cathy, the doctor still didn't admit that Carol's illness was fatal. What he said was that hospice could take care of her until she was strong enough to come back for more treatment.

Carol tried hospice for one day and, because she was still searching for a cure, she decided that it wasn't for her. She could get stronger on her own. So she flew up to Massachusetts to be with her family until she could resume treatment. She died three months later.

Carol didn't have a bad death. She made choices. She lived fully and she was well cared for by her family and friends. She did not die alone in the hospital; in fact, in the last month of her life she did hook up with a hospice program and died at home with her sister at her side. But she certainly received a lot of very invasive treatment that was of questionable value along the way. She suffered a lot of unnecessary pain and disability. She focused only on being cured. And her primary doctor apparently failed to give her clear information about what was happening, what her choices were, and what the future held. He talked about cures when the other doctors said it wasn't possible; he referred her to hospice but suggested it was a way "to get stronger"; he talked about treatments when none were available.

Carol wanted to fight her disease aggressively and so she sought out a doctor who could give her every weapon available. The doctor, in turn, fed her hope that those weapons would be effective and that more weapons stood in wait. Carol believed him and used everything he offered. She didn't press for more information and he didn't give it to her. A week before she died, Carol turned to her sister and said, "I should have read more about this death and dying stuff."

"If you told Carol five years ago that she was going to do all this she would have said, 'No way. I'm *not* going to have it dragged out like that,'" Cathy said. "She said a couple of times, 'If this chemo doesn't work, that's it. This is ridiculous.' And then she'd do the next one. . . . Her oncologist always had something else up his sleeve. I don't know if this was a game they were playing or not. I remember thinking, 'He's not serving Carol.' But who knows? Maybe that's what was best for her."

where is "there"?

by waiting, we often miss the boat

Repeatedly people have said to me that they don't need to question the value of aggressive or experimental treatments, they don't need to consider hospice care, they don't need to think about, much less do anything about, legacies or wills or comfort care or apologies or forgiveness, because they have not crossed that line. They are not at that point. They are not there, not yet.

Along with balancing hope, we must also be careful not to wait to be "there"—that place where we recognize and respond to the likelihood of death—for such a moment, such a clear turning point between fighting illness and preparing for death, rarely occurs. We must not wait because by the time we determine that we are "there," at that magical border, we have, quite often, missed our chance.

*　*　*

I am eavesdropping on a small circle of doctors, medical trainees, and nurses who are standing beside the nurses' station in a hospital intensive care unit. They are discussing whether or not to put a 77-year-old woman with end-stage emphysema and a weak heart on a ventilator. They are facing the woman's room, separated from her only by a large glass window. But they do not look at her. Instead, they listen intently to each other, study their notepads, and glance occasionally at a computer screen that holds her medical history and statistics from the machines that monitor her body's operations.

The woman's bed is in an upright position, but she is slumped down, her frail body sunken into the fold of the bed. Her head hangs to one side, too heavy for her to hold up. She appears small and much older than her years. Her white hair is wispy and disheveled, her face aged by sickness, pain, and exhaustion. A chalk-blue hospital gown falls loosely on her bony shoulders, revealing the upper part of her chest, a translucent map of veins and liver spots. Her thin arms, embedded by intravenous lines and monitors, shake and tremble wildly as she struggles to breathe. She cannot hear the discussion that is going on, but she stares at the group of men and women in white coats before her, her eyes frightened and searching for help.

According to the machines, she is getting enough oxygen, but the sensation of not getting enough air, of not being able to draw in a full breath, is making her panic. With some effort, she lifts her head and looks frantically at the doctors, waggling one shaky finger in a futile attempt to get their attention as they mull over her future.

Several members of the team are reluctant to intubate her because they doubt that she will ever get off the ventilator once she is put on it; such patients often become dependent upon the machine and then have trouble breathing on their own. One doctor explains that if she could only calm down she would not need "the vent." It is fear, not a shortage of oxygen, that has her in this state. But, he goes on, they cannot give her sedatives to calm her because the drugs would further jeopardize her ability to breathe. Other members of the team argue that she should be hooked up immediately "to ease her suffering." Keeping her off the machine is cruel. Who knows, they say. She might get off the vent at some point, and maybe even back home. It's not probable, they concede, but "in theory," it is possible.

The woman has a Do-Not-Resuscitate order in her chart indicating her wishes to be allowed to die should her heartbeat or breathing stop, but neither have stopped, and according to her nurse, intubation is not addressed; only manual chest compressions are specifically forbidden.

A member of the team says that when the woman's children were asked what should be done, they said not to intubate her. (There is no family member here at this time; they have been contacted by phone.) But when the patient herself was asked about being put on a ventilator, she said yes. One doctor and a nurse from the group feel that this is all they need to go on. She wants it, give it to her. The others aren't sure what to make of her response because she is confused and says yes to almost every question put to her.

The discussion goes on until a decision is made to not make a decision. They will wait. They will hold off on the ventilator for another day and then decide. Twenty-four hours later, the group reconvenes, but there is no new information to help them. The woman is the same, only more exhausted and more anxious. And so they decide to wait another day. No one even suggested that someone might simply sit with her, hold her hand, and offer gentle reassurance.

Was this the time to stop the fight and let her die peacefully? Was she "dying"? Should her children have come rushing in to say goodbye? Should a local hospice have been called? Or not? This scene, which is not uncommon, raises a number of issues, but the point is that managing death is not a simple thing, primarily because we don't know when to start that process. The words we use to describe our cut-off point, words like "hopeless," "beyond recovery," "futile," and "dying," are often meaningless when such a decision must actually be made. In most cases, illness and treatment decisions do not involve such absolutes. The prognosis is largely guesswork. Further treatment holds some promise, however remote. The patient's competency is questionable. And what will best confer comfort—life support or some other measure of care—is a matter of opinion.

We think, as we put ink to our living wills or make promises to our loved ones, that we won't end up on machines, lingering on the edge of life. We won't continue brutal treatments that hold little hope. We look at other people's horrific deaths and insist that *we* will never end up like that. *Our* loved ones won't die like that. We've signed the papers or voiced our wishes or made our promises. We know what we will do when the question is put to us: "Do you want to drag this out with some painful, invasive procedure that is essentially futile, or do you want to let her die peacefully?"

The problem is that the question is rarely so black and white. Dying is a complicated affair that involves multiple shades of gray. As medicine has developed more weapons, more ways of battling disease and keeping people alive, and more ways of fighting disturbing side effects, the question of when to stop has become more and more confusing. Quite often, there is no definitive moment when invasive procedures should be abandoned for palliative care, no unmistakable border between beneficial and futile, no turning point when a person goes from "living" to "dying." Today, people can live for years with terminal illness, suffering occasional scrapes with death and then rebounding.

As a patient inches his way across this uncertain terrain of illness and disability, there is usually some chance, however slim, that a treatment will help in some way, that the person will get a little better, or at least get worse more slowly. There is often some experimental treatment or alternative therapy that offers hope. And there is almost always some success story, some unusual patient who beat the odds, recovered, came back to life, spoke again, walked, lived longer than others.

Patients and families expect clear markers. We want to be told when it is time, without a doubt, to stop and switch tracks. But medicine doesn't have any such answers. Better statistical tools and computer programs have helped some, but still, doctors don't know when death will occur and they often don't know for sure whether further treatment will be of any use. They can give pretty good timelines with cancer, but not with many other life-threatening diseases. They can talk only of past experience and probabilities. And those probabilities are anything but simple.

In a paper describing how doctors might better predict survival times and then relay that information to patients, the authors, who were part of the large SUPPORT study, presented this scenario: Mr. Jones has lung disease and has made it clear that when death grows near, he doesn't want to be put on a ventilator. So the doctor sits him down to give him some information. He explains that, given his current condition, Mr. Jones has a 50 percent chance of dying within two months, a 10 percent chance of living for six months, a 1 percent chance of living a full year, and a 10 percent chance of dying in the next ten days. In light of these statistics, would Mr. Jones want to be hooked up to life-sustaining equipment if he becomes short of breath?

Obviously, this is not the sort of question poor Mr. Jones expected.

The crazy percentages involved reveal only part of the predicament, because tossed into this statistical stew are real people with real emotions. We are analyzing the probabilities and making decisions, sometimes for ourselves but usually for a loved one, when our hearts are heavy, our disbelief is paralyzing, and our instinctual desire to hang on is at full throttle. Imagine it. Your 74-year-old father is lying in a hospital bed, extremely ill. You've never had as close a relationship as you wanted, but you love him dearly and you aren't ready to give up your quest for some resolution or understanding. You need time with him. You don't want to let him go. Or maybe it's your wife lying there, or your sister. She's only 40 and she has young children at home. Or maybe the person in that bed is a child, your child, a tiny, sweet-faced boy whom you adore with every cell of your body. What are you going to do when the doctor says that a particular treatment has a 70 percent chance of extending life several months, but that it might cause unpleasant side effects, like nausea, cramping, infections? Would you agree to it? What if the treatment had only a 20 percent chance of prolonging life and the side effects were more severe? What if the treatment might extend life only another few weeks, rather than months? What about using a treatment that is so new that the probabilities and side effects are unknown? How far are you willing to go? How much pain is acceptable? What odds are worth pursuing? At what point would you say stop?

As long as a treatment holds some hope of doing something, as long as one statistic seems favorable, as long as there is one example of someone who beat the odds, how does a person ever say no? How do you ever stop treatment? The fact is, most of us don't. We push ahead, pursuing one treatment after another, waiting to come upon some proclamation that "nothing more can be done." But instead, the odds just get slimmer and the costs more burdensome, and we keep on fighting because we are not "there." Not yet.

Although we say that we don't want "extraordinary means," by most any definition, that is what we get. We forge ahead and then either the patient dies during the course of treatment, or the family finally seeks palliative care, but only after the patient has suffered terribly and is no longer nearing death or preparing to die, but is actively dying. He is bedridden, dependent, and only partially conscious. Now there will be no closure, resolution, or legacies. There will be little more than heavy narcotics to see him through the end.

Daniel Callahan, director of the Hastings Center, a medical ethics think tank, calls this habit of waiting, this desire to get as close to zero return as possible, "technological brinkmanship." "Common sense seems to dictate such a course," he says in his book *The Troubled Dream of Life*. "Aggressively work to prolong life until it becomes futile, or harmful, to continue doing so; then, just as boldly, halt life-extending treatment. But this seemingly obvious strategy assumes an ability to manage technology and its consequences with a delicacy and precision that medicine simply does not possess and may never possess."

We wait because it is too painful to accept that someone is dying, and because we don't want to miss out on a treatment that might, just possibly, prolong life. And we wait because we never anticipated the questions, never understood the issues, and never prepared ourselves to call such difficult shots. Suddenly, standing beside someone we love, minuscule odds and physical suffering seem better than no chance at all. And saying "stop" when we've had no preparation to do so is nearly impossible.

Obviously, we cannot wait to be "there," at some neat boundary between "living" and "dying." We have to accept that we are already "there" as soon as we or someone we love has a potentially terminal disease. We are "there" throughout an illness, focusing on life but also preparing for the possibility of death. We are "there," making choices and taking actions that affect how we will live and how we, or our loved ones, will ultimately die.

Even if a person is still seeking a cure, and certainly when no cure is possible, we need to have our visits, write our notes, open our hearts, and be with him. We need to be aware, always, that we simply don't know what's going to happen, or when. And therefore, we can't wait. Certain things must not be put off, for there may be no second chances.

People worry that addressing problems in a relationship or expressing one's love or thanks casts undue gravity on the situation (*If I do that he will think that I think that he is going to die*). The fact is, the situation is serious, even if it is not fatal, so a little gravity is all right.

If we are going to avoid this waiting game, we also need to realize that each time we make a decision about drugs or scans or radiation or surgery, we are charting a course. With each decision we gain something and give something up and we affect the final outcome. With each incremental step, we need to ask difficult but critical questions: Why are we doing this? What are we trying to achieve? What are we losing in the process? When will we stop? And how can we prepare ourselves for what lies ahead?

Two stories help illustrate this point:

A 95-year-old man with severe dementia is hooked to a dozen tubes and IV lines—a ventilator, heart monitors, antibiotic lines, feeding tube. He is only questionably alive, has little hope of getting better, and has no hope of ever going home. His case begs the question: "Why?" The nurse explains to me that despite his dementia, this man had been reasonably healthy. He was living with his son when one day he walked into the kitchen for a bite to eat and fell and broke his hip. He was brought into the hospital for hip surgery, after which he aspirated (sucked stomach juices into his lungs), developed pneumonia, and risked developing a systemic, life-threatening infection, which is how he ended up like this.

Where could things have turned a different way? Considering his age, his disease, his future, and the risks of surgery, could the man have foregone the surgery and stayed in bed, comfortably, until he died? I raised this question with a highly respected orthopedic surgeon and he responded, aghast, "Oh no. You've got to give him the surgery. You might get him back on his feet again."

The second story involves Angela Scott and her mother, Margaret, who is in the late stages of Alzheimer's disease. Margaret lives with Angela and her husband, and requires constant supervision. She can't walk or eat or go to the bathroom without assistance. Most of the time she doesn't know where she is or who anyone else is or what she is doing or why she is doing it. But she doesn't seem to be in any pain or distress. She is cared for meticulously and lovingly, and appears calm and content.

Several years ago a doctor started Margaret on a drug that was expected to slow the progress of her disease and, at the time, it seemed to be helping. But now that Margaret is so acutely ill, her daughter wonders if the drug serves any purpose. The doctor has told Angela that Margaret should continue the drug because it might still be slowing the progress of the disease. But Angela remains uncertain. She turned to me one day and explained her angst. "Why," she asked me, with a look of guilt, "would I want to slow her disease?"

I tell these stories not to suggest that these patients should or should not have received the treatments they did, but to point out how uncomfortable people are with the questions that are raised. And yet, these are exactly the kind of questions that we must ask. What are our goals? What will happen if we stop? What sort of life, and death, might this person have? We must ask these questions because they are pertinent. We must ask them because we are "there." We must ask them, as people never have before, because although medicine has not beaten death, it has transformed it. Drastically.

We are entering a new era in which we must decide not simply *whether* to quit, but *when* to quit. We are not just deciding whether or not to prolong death, but how we might make the most of the end of life. We are not simply deciding whether or not to keep a dying person on a ventilator, but whether we will accept the ventilator in the first place, whether we will proceed with a treatment, or whether we will even call an ambulance when things get rough. In other words, we are no longer deciding simply whether life is viable, but whether it is desirable.

Now that medicine can take us further than ever before, it is up to us, as individuals, to decide how far we want to go. We have to ask the questions and then decide: When do the burdens of a treatment outweigh the benefits? What level of pain is bearable? What degree of confusion is tolerable? What sorts of disabilities are acceptable? When do we want to stop treatment and instead make the best of whatever life remains? Rather than waiting for the point of zero return to switch tracks, we have to actually look for opportunities, for openings, to make death peaceful. We have to look for moments when we can still find comfort and make death more gentle.

Will we be haunted by doubts if we opt for palliative care before invasive care is deemed "futile?" *What if we had kept going? What if we had pushed harder? What if we had chosen the surgery, the chemotherapy, the ventilator?* Of course we will. Until we get used to this new assignment, until we fully understand and accept what death is today and how we might influence it, we will wonder. But we also have to consider what we might have lost if we had kept on pushing the envelope, opting for more treatment, more days in the ICU, more pain.

None of this is going to be easy, but then no one said it would be. Medicine has brought us to a new place, and we have to respond by asking difficult questions, weighing confusing options, and making excruciating decisions that people have never had to consider before.

rosemary's story

It is late January in New York City and the air outside is cold and cheerless. The air on the seventh floor of Lenox Hill Hospital, where I have spent much of the afternoon, is stale and smells vaguely of urine and antiseptics. The hallway is cluttered with meal carts, linen carts, wheelchairs, and blood pressure machines, so it takes a lot of maneuvering to stay out of the way of the nurses, aides, and orderlies who brush by. I am waiting here in this hallway because a family is about to talk with a doctor about their mother's diagnosis and treatment options. It is one moment in a lengthy illness. It is a conference that occurs many times a day in every hospital in this country. Five siblings file quietly into the hospital's "family lounge" ahead of me.

Their mother, whom I will call Rosemary for the sake of privacy, is 73 years old. She has been failing here and there for more than a year—cataract surgery, headaches, inexplicable abdominal pain, foot pain, forgetfulness, loneliness, and a declining interest in life. Over the past year, she sold her summer cottage, signed a will and advance directives, bought long-term care insurance, and squirreled herself away in her uptown apartment.

A few days prior to this meeting, she became delirious, fell and broke her pelvis, and was hospitalized. Several days of tests revealed that she has a rare disease called multiple myeloma, a cancer of the blood plasma that cripples the immune system, decimates bones, and wreaks havoc in the kidneys. It seems that the cancer was responsible for her previous headaches and foot pain, as it can cause tumors in the bone. The doctors suspect that she also had a stroke, leading to her current state of confusion.

Now her children sit on toothpaste-blue vinyl chairs, facing one another uncomfortably, as a young doctor glances at his notes and outlines the facts, most of which they already know. Rosemary's cancer is stage three, advanced. While there is no cure, chemotherapy might slow the progression of the disease. The news, while expected, is devastating nonetheless.

The doctor recommends a type of chemo that is given through a portal, or permanent opening, in her chest. The drug combination is milder than most and shouldn't cause the usual hair loss and nausea, but it does require that she come into the hospital for four days each month. He drones on, reeling out statistics and opinions, flipping pages in his notebook back and forth. Clearly, he wants to help, to say the right thing, but he is desperately awkward and uncomfortable here, in the midst of all this silent despair. The average life span, with treatment, he says, reciting from his notes, is two to five years. Without treatment, people live an average of 15 months. Of course, these statistics include people much younger and healthier than Rosemary, so the time frame is likely to be shorter for her. In any case, the cancer eventually leads to infections, bone fractures, and kidney failure. In addition to all of this, Rosemary's pelvis is not healing well and it is not clear how much mobility she will regain, if any. And her confusion, which now has her drifting along the edges of lucidity, is not likely to improve significantly.

On the face of it, the choice seems obvious: the family feels that they should at least try the chemo, to see if it will help. No one has presented any other choice, and various consulting doctors have expressed some surprise that the treatment hasn't been started already.

But the siblings don't want to rush into anything. Some don't want to miss out on a valuable treatment—indeed, they are asking about experimental treatments and more aggressive approaches. She was well just the other day; there must be some way to return to that place. Others are concerned because they don't want to make their mother suffer needlessly, and they don't want to subject her to something that she wouldn't want. Rosemary has stated quite clearly in the past that she would not want chemotherapy if she had terminal cancer. But no one is sure why she didn't want it. This treatment shouldn't cause the side effects that may have scared her in the past. It does require, however, that she return to the hospital each month, which, given her current state, seems like a formidable task.

As the siblings contemplate all of this, their mother lies in a "semi-private" room down the hall, her skin grayed, her eyes dulled, her hair limp, and her movements slow and deliberate. She recognizes visitors, but then watches with little expression as the conversation in her room goes on without her. It's not clear how much, if any, of it she grasps. "Let's go upstairs to my room where we can be alone," she mutters suddenly. "My room is empty." Later she talks about a party she's going to, a walk she's taken, a new house she's moved into—none of which has happened or is about to happen. Perhaps she is delirious; perhaps she is aware of the trip she has embarked on here.

On the one hand, she still finds joy in being with her children and grandchildren and her confusion seems to have her, while not in this world, at least in a happy place. On the other hand, she is bedridden, incontinent and disoriented, headed, it seems, toward only more disability and discomfort. Is chemotherapy the right option if it promises only to keep her in this state for a little longer than she might otherwise?

The children think their mother should decide about the chemotherapy for herself, but there is some question as to whether she is
lucid enough to make such a decision. She has named her son as her
health care proxy, but no one can agree upon whether that power has
passed into his hands yet. One doctor says she is not competent to
make decisions for herself; another says that perhaps she is. And,
indeed, at times she is and at times she isn't.

The children wait until a more lucid moment and put the question
to her. But both because of her exhaustion and because of her nature,
she tells them to decide. "I guess I should have the chemotherapy," she
says wearily, and then adds, "What do all of you think? You decide."

And so, they are back to where they started, conferring over their
mother's future, asking questions about treatments, weighing the quality of life against the quantity of life. If the chemotherapy gives her an
extra few months or even a year, what will that time be like? If she is
so confused that she doesn't know where she is, if she can't get up
much less out, if she can't read the books that she loves, if she needs
24-hour care from strangers, what kind of life will they have given
her? Will she be in pain? Will her bones become so brittle that they
break at every turn? Will she need dialysis? Will living in the hospital for four days of every month be bearable? Is there some point at
which she might have to be in the hospital for longer stretches? In the
end, will the chemotherapy give her more life, or will it only give her
more days of discomfort, devouring precious time with its toxicity?

They don't know what to do. But they do recognize that they are
"there," trying to give their mother the longest life, but also the best
possible death. They do not want to plunge forward with treatment,
waiting blindly for some future moment when the answers are obvious
and the opportunities gone. They are "there," making horrendous
decisions that people never had to make before, but that are becoming common in our time.

taking the blame

we are not the cause of death

One of the reasons we keep going, keep opting for more treatment under the most dire circumstances, is that we feel unduly responsible. We feel that if we reject a particular treatment, we are not simply allowing death to come, we are *causing* it. This feeling of culpability is yet another obstacle that we need to examine carefully and anticipate.

When Ruth Sullivan fell and broke her hip at age 89, she recovered remarkably well. Within weeks of her surgery, she was up and walking, using her cane for balance, and living back in her apartment with minimal outside help. This came as no surprise to those who knew her. Ruth was always spry and active. She had played golf until she was 87, and had walked two to three miles every day for as long as anyone could remember. But despite her rapid recovery, Ruth was not happy about her less mobile, more dependent state, and her frustration and depression were evident.

About a month after her fall, Ruth was eating lunch in the dining room at her "senior" apartment building when she went into cardiac arrest. She was rushed to the emergency room and a medical team jolted her heart back into action. Although she had a living will saying that she did not want to be on life support, the emergency crew knew nothing about it and would never risk losing a life to ask about such a thing. Their job is to save patients' lives. They respond to the situation, and they respond urgently.

Ruth was revived and connected to a ventilator and other machines and monitors. During this procedure, which is not just frantic, but brutal, her trachea—the pipe leading from the nose and mouth into the lungs—was punctured and later had to be surgically repaired, and her ability to swallow was impaired. Within weeks she dropped from 122 to 93 pounds. She couldn't speak because the ventilator blocked her mouth.

Ruth's niece and namesake, Ruth Sullivan, went to the hospital as soon as she heard what had happened. "When we got there, there were tubes coming out of everywhere," she recalls. "We thought, 'Oh my God, this is what she's always dreaded. I can't believe we have let this happen to her.'"

Two days later, the elder Ruth, still in the I.C.U., began bleeding internally. She needed a transfusion and she needed it fast. At that moment, she was still hooked to life support and was only marginally cognizant. She couldn't speak and didn't recognize people. Her niece said she looked wild and afraid. Her family—two nieces and one nephew—had to make a decision quickly. The transfusion procedure was not complicated. They merely had to give her large amounts of blood over the course of several hours through an IV into her arm. But she was old, she had serious heart damage, and she wasn't going to get much better even with a transfusion. Almost no one at her age and particularly in her health lives more than a year after resuscitation. It was very likely that there would be other problems, more decline, and additional complications. The doctor explained that at this point, the staff could make her comfortable and that without the transfusion death would probably occur within two or three days. Ruth, the niece, remembers that the doctor even hinted that this might be a good time to let her aunt go, but she also made it clear that the decision was up to the family.

"My brother, sister, and I spent so long talking and crying," Ruth said. "We were trying to separate ourselves and what we wanted—we obviously wanted her to live, we wanted to talk to her again—from what she would want. We were trying to decide, if she were conscious, what she would say. And we knew in our hearts what that was. Definitely. I had had a talk with her just two weeks before and she had said, 'I want to go. I want to die. I've been here too long. I don't know why I'm still around. All of my friends are gone. I've had enough.' She had told everyone in the family this."

It was a horrendous decision to have to make. Each minute seemed critical. She could die at any moment. Procrastination would *be* a decision. A team was standing by, ready to begin the transfusion. The pressure was enormous. The siblings had to choose.

They knew what Aunt Ruth would have wanted. They knew what they should do. And yet, they simply could not do it. They didn't want to lose her, that was certainly behind their final decision to proceed with more treatment. But beyond that, they were haunted by a feeling that they were not simply allowing death, but causing it. By forgoing the transfusion, they were not simply letting nature take its course or keeping their beloved aunt comfortable; they were murdering her.

"You feel like, if you don't do it, you're killing her, taking some sort of determined action to end her life," Ruth said.

The transfusion was performed. And to illustrate just how complicated these decisions can be, here is what happened to Aunt Ruth: she recovered well enough to leave the hospital and spend Thanksgiving with her nieces and nephew, which was a gift. But shortly after that, she fell and broke her other hip. She developed pneumonia, became delirious, got a bowel infection, became incontinent, got a urinary tract infection, and her legs swelled to enormous proportions from edema. She wasn't eating. She became dehydrated. Her heart was failing. She was in terrible, terrible pain.

Ruth asked repeatedly to die. But it wasn't happening. "I should be up there," she would say. Once she said, "Just take me out and shoot me. I mean it, Ruthie. I've had enough."

Two months later, Ruth died. The week before, she was moved from the hospital into a nursing home, where she refused all medications. Family members spent the weekend by her bedside, talking to her about what she'd meant to them, how they felt about her, and praying with her. Her favorite nurse was with her when she took her final breath.

The point isn't whether or not Ruth should have had the transfusion, for there is no clearly right answer. The point is that when we are asked to make decisions about care at the end of life, we sometimes opt for continued treatment, despite our better judgment, because we feel like executioners. We don't want to say good-bye and we can't help but hope for miracles, but we also feel that if we reject treatment we will be personally responsible for the death of a loved one. This feeling not only hinders our decisions, but haunts us for years to come.

Ruth's situation was a bit hazy perhaps, for a transfusion is a fairly simple procedure and it was sure to get her over a hump. On the other hand, she was going to die soon one way or another and this was an opportunity for her to slip away easily. In any case, the shadow of culpability was there, affecting the decision, and it exists even when the decisions are more clear-cut. I've seen this not only in my research, but in my personal life. My mother felt guilty because she gave my father morphine in his dying days and she thought that his death came sooner because of it. My husband felt responsible because he accepted hospice care for his mother, even though the doctor recommended it and said that further treatment was futile. And a friend, who asked that his name not be used, felt horrible when he decided to remove his mother from life support.

His mother was in her seventies and extremely active and independent when she suddenly had massive bleeding in her brain due to a ruptured aneurysm. After surgeons stopped the bleeding, she lay, unresponsive, hooked to breathing, feeding, and hydrating tubes; heart monitors, oxygen monitors, and the rest, for three months. Finally, her doctor told the family that she would never get off the machines, she would never recover. Her husband and children decided, reluctantly, to take her off the machinery and let her die.

"It's creepy to be able to control these things," my friend said in the midst of the ordeal, while he was still contemplating what to do. "The whole thing makes me sick. . . . I don't care what anybody says, you are taking actions that will effectively end her life. We were causing her death."

He is right. No one should have to make such a decision. But we do. The vast majority of deaths today occur after such decisions are made. And the more medicine offers us, the more common and the more difficult these decisions will become.

But my friend is also wrong. He and his family did not cause his mother's death. And this is where we have to start making changes, in our attitudes and understanding about what death is and how it occurs and what role we play in it. People should feel an enormous sense of responsibility, for these are major decisions, but they should not feel personally responsible for death itself; they should feel only responsible for finding a way toward the most humane death. We have to get away from our guilt-ridden mind-set, and to see all these issues in a different light.

We should start with our language. We talk about "giving up" and "letting go." We talk about cases being "hopeless" and about "pulling the plug." We talk about "futility" and about "ending treatment." We talk about "doing everything" versus "doing nothing." We talk about "aggressive care," which suggests that the alternative is less aggressive, or perhaps not "care" at all.

When we take a terminally ill patient off life support, we are not "pulling the plug," we are "freeing" the patient to die. We are "releasing" her from excessive technology and invasive treatments. When we allow death to happen, we are not killing people, we are caring for them. We are loving them. We are respecting nature and all that life and death are about. We are taking them from medicine's iron grip, swaddling them in our arms, kissing their ashen cheeks, and, as we summon all of our strength, giving them the most generous gift of all: we are letting them go. This is not an act of murder. It is an act of love.

in the land of doctors

navigating the medical terrain

The final word of warning brings us back, full circle, to the doctors—the doctors who, in their valiant effort to maintain life, often distort death. The caution offered here, however, is not about the doctors per se, but rather our views and expectations of them.

Most of us follow our doctors somewhat blindly. We trust them. We feel safe around them. We become a little meek and obsequious in their presence. When serious illness strikes and we are feeling vulnerable and frightened, our doctors become almost godlike. They enter the room and we don't want them to leave. Their mere presence makes us feel better. We put them in charge. We let them, directly or indirectly, guide not only our care, but our perceptions, hopes, and responses. We do it because we don't know what else to do. And we do it because they have training, experience, contacts, and tools—perhaps lifesaving tools—that we don't.

But if we are going to change the way we die, we need to rethink this attitude, or at least be keenly attuned to it. For as much as we might trust and respect our doctors, we also need to recognize that they have limits and biases, and that death is not their friend. We need to ask direct questions, be willing to disagree with them, and get second opinions. We need, ultimately, to accept responsibility for our own care and the care of our loved ones.

an imperfect profession

Obviously there are many doctors who handle the end of life beautifully, doctors who can look into the eyes of a dying person and share his pain, doctors who can sit patiently with a troubled family and assuage their grief, doctors who take end-of-life care as seriously as they take life-saving care. I have met some of these men and women. I watched as one listened calmly and compassionately to a family who refused to accept a terminal diagnosis, and then, over the course of a week, ever so gently helped them to come to terms with what was happening. One sat at a bedside for several hours holding a young patient's hand until he died. One taught frightened family members how to speak to and gently massage a loved one who was dying. These are the true miracle workers, who understand the science of medicine, the art of communication, and the intricacies of the human soul.

All too often, however, doctors fail dying patients and their families. As our guides along this final path, they often lead us in a direction we never intended to go, or desert us just when we need them most. Studies show that doctors often delay or avoid breaking bad news; they use euphemisms and jargon when speaking with gravely ill patients; they minimize the severity of an illness and give patients undue hope; they knowingly overtreat patients who are terminally ill; and they spend dramatically less time with patients once those patients are known to be "dying."

We cannot make informed decisions if we don't have proper information. We cannot forgo senseless treatments, seek hospice care, or achieve any sort of a peaceful death if we do not know that the treatments are senseless, that hospice is an option, or that death is approaching. We cannot be anything but afraid and anxious if our doctors desert us in the final hour.

Ben Holden, as you may recall from "A Portrait of Death," was lying in his hospital bed when his doctor walked in, said that Ben had "a real bad booger" in his esophagus and not much time left, and then walked out. One woman told me that she didn't hear anything at all from her doctor after cancer spread into her spine and hip; after eight months of treating her with experimental drugs, he simply contacted her primary physician and said, "You can take care of her now."

Even doctors who are praised by their colleagues for their ability to deal with dying patients sometimes use questionable tactics. I caught up with one such doctor as he was emerging from the room of a patient who was close to death. She was having trouble breathing, a frightening symptom. He had just asked her whether she wanted to be put on a ventilator. When I asked what other option he offered her, he replied gravely, "She knows the other option."

I doubt that she did. She was suffering and he had suggested a way to relieve that suffering. His words—or his lack of words—implied that her other option was to suffocate until she died. He did not tell her that the ventilator would mean not only that she couldn't eat, talk, or cough, but that she would have to be fed and hydrated mechanically, and that she would have to have secretions suctioned out of her lungs regularly. He did not explain to her that there were other ways to ease her discomfort—sedatives, painkillers, oxygen, bronchodilators, fluid reduction, and, if anyone had the time, human contact and tenderness. He did not tell her that once her anxiety passed, she might go on breathing on her own for some time. He did not tell her that, in the end, death was the only option, but that there were several ways to get there.

Another doctor highly regarded by his colleagues for his honesty in these issues had a patient whose cancer had spread to eleven different areas of his brain. Chemotherapy and radiation no longer held any promise; it was time to focus on comfort. And yet, according to one colleague, the doctor kept softening anything he said with words like "yet" or "at this time." So the family kept asking, "Is it time for more chemo *yet*?" The doctor admitted privately that he was hoping the patient would decide against further chemotherapy, which would end the discussion and put the weight of this decision on the patient's shoulders, rather than on his or the family's.

Doctors often tiptoe around the subject of death, talking instead about long-term survival rates, remission, and effective treatments. They talk about patients who have "expired" and diseases that are "not compatible with life." (I have actually heard that expression used more than once.) They blame patients for not wanting to talk about death when often it is the doctor who is avoiding the subject. And all too frequently they refer to life-sustaining and other invasive treatments as "comfort care," treating patients "palliatively" with intravenous fluids, feeding tubes, antibiotics, and ventilators. One doctor, standing next to a human pincushion in an ICU, said to me, "I told the family that we can unhook him and let him die, or we can continue to keep him comfortable." This is comfort?

It's not that doctors are unfeeling. They don't walk past the doors of their dying patients or speak in techno-tongue or pursue futile treatments because they are malicious. I am not even convinced that they do it because they want to make an extra buck or because they want to avoid lawsuits, as some people argue. Most doctors are simply responding to an incredibly difficult situation in the best way they know how.

"Part of what you're supposed to do is help people die as well as they can. That's part of the job," says Dr. Elizabeth Beautyman (the internist at Roosevelt Hospital in New York). "But it is *extremely* difficult to walk into a patient's room in the hospital, a patient who is dying, but is not dead yet. There is no treatment. You're just waiting for them to die and they're waiting to die. You walk in and say, 'How are things today, Mr. Jones?' It's very difficult. . . . You aren't sure what they want from you, and you don't know what to give them."

Doctors are only human. They are dealing with their own fears of death, and their own ignorance about end-of-life care. They are responding to cues from individual patients and their families, and they are also responding to strong pressures from society to treat, to save, to do more. The way doctors deal with patients and families reflects years of training, established medical routines, growing fiscal pressures, and a system that values invasive, life-sustaining treatments over time-consuming palliative care and counseling.

the training process

Young, eager college graduates enter medical school with good intentions and compassionate hearts. They want to help people. They want to alleviate suffering. They want to combat disease. But during those first two years of school, medical students are so inundated by technical details, biological minutiae, and pages of facts that rote memorization and getting through each exam becomes their only concern.

The patient is reduced to a set of hormones, genes, blood cells, and a list of mechanical failures. He is no longer a person, but a "host," an environment within which diseases reside and troubles occur. Students are taught how to fix faulty valves, fight bacterial invaders, remove damaged tissue, jump-start faltering hearts, and close wounds. The patient as a car; the hospital as a body shop; the doctor as a mechanic. Little time in medical school is spent discussing the patient as a person, much less the patient's needs, fears, comfort, or quality of life. Even less time is spent talking about how to help patients die.

A recent survey showed that only 6 of the 126 medical schools in the United States have a separate, required course on end-of-life care; the other 120 include the subject as part of some other course. (In Canada, all 16 medical schools require students to study palliative care, but the entire subject is usually covered in less than 11 hours.) The subject is sneaking, ever so slowly, into the course load, but still, it is given in dribs and drabs. It is not incorporated into the heart of medical education. It is not treated as if it were a routine and valued part of medicine. It is handled as something separate and unusual. Those courses that exist are not part of the core curriculum and, in many cases, are taught not by doctors, but by nurses, social workers, medical ethicists, and chaplains.

"We have faculty who teach classes, who tell them this is important," says Dr. Robert Levine, professor of medicine at the Yale University School of Medicine. "But what we don't have is a solid body of role models who don't just say it's important, but do it as if it were important."

When students finally pull their noses out of their books and begin to deal with human subjects, usually in the third year of medical school, they spend their time with patients who are receiving treatment and are expected to recover, not patients who are dying.

Dr. R. Sean Morrison, a geriatrician at Mount Sinai Medical Center in New York, recalls: "In four years of medical school, I saw one person die and that was unexpected, on the operating table. The doctor walked out, spent two minutes with the man's friend who had brought him in, and left."

A survey of medical students in the United States found that while all third-year medical students had cared for at least one patient who was dying, 41 percent had never heard a doctor talking with a dying patient, 35 percent had never discussed care for dying patients with a senior doctor, and half the students couldn't remember anything in their course curriculum that dealt with end-of-life care.

Not only do students receive inadequate training on how to talk to and care for terminally ill patients, but during those early years most of them learn to distance themselves from these patients. They become a bit callous, not because they are evil but because they are human. Medical students work long, exhausting days and nights under enormous pressures, and they witness extraordinary pain— hourly. They are surrounded by patients who are oozing, defecating, moaning, and decaying. They see people's bodies splayed open, ripped apart, and withering away. And they see families crushed by unimaginable anxiety and grief. It is difficult and frightening, and so the students steel themselves and separate themselves, the young and healthy, from the sick.

Quite simply, allowing yourself to care about someone who is likely to die, hurts. "There's a fine line between getting to know a patient and staying back so you don't break down when something happens," explained a student who took a seminar at Yale's School of Medicine on caring for dying patients. "It's putting yourself through an emotional wringer," another student said. "You're going to become friends with somebody who's going to die."

Yes, and they are going to do it over and over again. So to survive, they try not to become too close or to care too much. They turn from the hurt, and focus their energy on physical healing.

After medical school, students begin their "residency," which is on-the-job training. They choose a medical specialty, and then often a subspecialty, learning about cancer, for example, and then cancer of the blood and then treatments for a specific type of leukemia. As they zero in on a field of medicine and then a specific disease, organ, or mode of treatment, they move further away from any sort of holistic approach. They know about laproscopy or radiation or transplantation. They learn what's new and what's hot. They become human microscopes, focusing in on the minute and, in the process, sometimes losing sight of the whole.

My young son has a wonderful book called *Zoom*, in which each picture offers a broader view than the one before; the reader sees dots on a rooster's head, the rooster on a farm, the farm as a child's toy, the child and her toy as a picture in a magazine, and so on and so on, backing up in this way until the reader is looking at a dot which is Earth. Young doctors do just the opposite, zooming in, from humanity to a patient to an illness to an organ to a cell to a protein; zooming in, closer and closer, until there is no humanity, and no patient anymore. There is only a disease, a treatment, and a response.

down the halls of medicine

Whatever they have learned, or have not learned, in medical school, whatever protective armors or tunnel-vision they might have developed, once established in the medical system most doctors become fairly adept at walking the line between getting personally involved with patients and staying back so that they can get through the day. We can doctor-bash all we want, but the truth is that doctors want to help. They want to make things better. And they hurt when their patients are dying. Few doctors go into medicine purely for money or prestige. They care about their patients, even when those patients are known to be dying.

But it is this very determination to take care of patients and make things better that gets in the way of helping patients who are dying. Doctors want to fix things and save lives; that is why they go to medical school, that is what they are trained to do, and that is what they are rewarded for. They know that, in theory, every ailment is fixable, if only they could find the right tools. With a stronger drug or a newer treatment or a better procedure they should be able to decimate the cancer, manipulate the heart, assist the lungs, prevent the infection, repair the damage. It all makes sense. So they push forward, trying to solve the puzzle that illness presents, and to fend off, for as long as possible, the ultimate enemy—Death.

Many doctors are also driven by an inescapable belief that they can beat the odds because, tucked into the back of their minds, is an indelible memory of a patient who survived, or a patient for whom life beyond the edge was worthwhile. "They may have seen a 90-year-old man resuscitated successfully so that he could move back home for another six months or year of life," said Dr. Kenneth Prager from New York Presbyterian Hospital. "They may have seen someone put on a ventilator and then [removed from it and] sent home, debilitated and needing constant oxygen—perhaps in a state most of us couldn't bear—and observed him having meaningful time with children and grandchildren, and heard him say a thousand thank-yous for 'saving my life.' That memory can become a vivid image in a moment of crisis when someone is unable to breathe. The rest of us can say, especially after the person dies a horrible death, that this death was inescapable and the action unjustified, inhumane even. But for that doctor, it was not done to harm someone. It was done because there was a chance. An infinitesimally small chance maybe, but a chance."

When doctors know that they cannot make a patient better, many of them feel as if they have failed. No matter what the intellect might know—that this is not their fault—an inner voice haunts them: *Did I do all that I could have done? Was there something I should have done differently?* Thoughts of the patient, the life that was lost, haunt them. Thoughts of the family, who will be heartbroken, haunt them. Thoughts of their own training and career haunt them. The dying patient becomes a disturbing reflection not only of medicine's limits, but of the doctor's personal failings.

"A doctor is often torn by the feeling, 'I did the wrong thing, I gave the wrong drug, I shouldn't have done this operation, or maybe if I had somehow done it a little more meticulously there wouldn't have been this infection,'" says Dr. Sherwin Nuland, author of *How We Die*. "On some level, it's always my fault. On some level, I always let the family down, always let the patient down. . . . Doctors are a self-selected group," he continued, "and one of the characteristics we select for is obsessional thinking, compulsive behavior, a terrible sense of obligation, and punishing superegos. We blame ourselves for everything."

Other doctors say they don't feel that they have failed as much as they feel horribly helpless when a patient is dying. In the face of death, when the drugs and machines won't make someone better, when all that technical training is useless, they don't know what to do. They don't know how to help. They don't know what to say.

Of course, under all this fierce ambition and desire to help is a very human response to death. Doctors arrive at a bedside with their own fears of death, unresolved grief, and uncertainty about how to respond to someone else's loss. They are not sure how to bring up the subject or relay the facts. They get upset when a patient cries hysterically or falls silently into despair. They are uncomfortable with death just like the rest of us are.

Dr. Elisabeth Kübler-Ross, who has taught leagues of young doctors about death and dying, also found this to be true. "Those physicians who were most afraid of the issue of death and dying never revealed the truth to their patients, rationalizing that the patients were not willing to talk about it," she wrote in her book *To Live Until We Say Good-Bye.* "These professionals were not able to see the projection of their own fears, their hidden anxiety, yet the patients were able to pick up these feelings and, therefore, never shared their own knowledge with their physicians. This situation left many dying in a vacuum, unattended and lonely."

pressures from outside

In addition to the narrowness of medical education and the passions and fears of individual doctors, are the pressures, rewards, and deeply integrated routines of the workplace that have an enormous influence on how doctors care for patients who they know are going to die.

An unwavering drive to battle disease and prolong life is applauded and encouraged by hospital administrators and co-workers—and by society. The guy who pulls a patient through, who uses an innovative treatment, who is part of a leading research team, who is adept at using the newest technology, is a hero. He or she is published, given tenure, interviewed by the media, embraced by the patient and family, and revered by colleagues. When doctors get together to review cases, they discuss the patients who survived, the treatments that worked, the mistakes that were made; the question of whether or not a patient lived fully at the end or found a "good death" is not mentioned.

Dr. Howard Spiro, editor of the book *Facing Death*, says that death "rarely makes it to grand rounds: our mortality conferences review why someone has died and what errors may have been made, but we never wonder aloud whether it could have been the right time for that patient to die."

In medical circles, palliative care is neither well understood, nor highly respected. Although pain and symptom management has become a technically complex field, it is still widely considered to be "soft" medicine—medicine for sissies. In the United States, such specialized care is not even offered in many hospitals, and in those hospitals where palliative care programs do exist, doctors often don't understand what the units do and are reluctant to refer patients to them.

Tacked onto this are the same issues that guide and distort many professions today: lawsuits, rapidly advancing technology, and financial pressures.

It is unclear how much doctors are influenced by a fear of lawsuits when caring for terminally ill patients. Certainly, tests are ordered and procedures done, at least in part, to protect doctors from legal trouble. And random interviews suggest that many doctors still do not understand the laws regarding end-of-life care. Even though judges and medical societies have repeatedly upheld a patient's, and a legal surrogate's, right to refuse medical treatment, including life-sustaining treatment, doctors routinely question whether or not they can withdraw or withhold such treatment.

As for technology and medical innovation, it has not only complicated the decisions and allowed us to stretch out the final months and days of life, but it has also put us in the hands of strangers just when we need a familiar face. By the time people are seriously ill, they are often distanced from their family doctors, who knew not only their medical histories, but something of their personal histories. Instead, they are seeing a specialist—an oncologist, neurologist, hematologist, cardiologist, pulmonologist—or a team of specialists, who don't have a relationship with the patient or family and may not know the patient's wishes and priorities. Furthermore, patients are sometimes seeing these specialists and subspecialists and medical teams at a tertiary-care hospital—a cancer center, a heart and blood institute, a neurological clinic—which is several hours away from their home, family, and friends.

Finally, fiscal pressures have become an enormous intrusion. In this era of managed care, doctors who might like to spend a little time with a patient, who might like to develop some sort of relationship and understanding, are hard-pressed to do so. Instead, they are pressured to see a certain number of patients within a certain amount of time. A visit typically lasts about ten minutes, often less, which is barely enough time to say hello and how's your heart, much less talk about a person's wishes at the end of life, their personal goals, or their feelings about comfort care and counseling.

reexamining our expectations

Clearly, doctors need to learn how to relay bad news, and how to handle patients' responses of anger, despair, or denial. They need to learn how to initiate discussions about end-of-life care and to discuss all the options. They need to acknowledge the limits of medicine, understand the shifting nature of hope, and become more familiar with the laws and legal decisions regarding the rejection or refusal of treatment. And they definitely need to learn more about palliative care and witness all that it is possible to do at the end of life.

But we also have to be realistic. How much change can we expect from our doctors? And, quite honestly, how much change do we want?

Doctors will always be focused, first and foremost, on fighting illness and on saving lives. They are doctors, not therapists. They are trained, quite rigorously, to battle disease and extend life. That goal is drummed into their hearts and minds from the moment they take their first course in anatomy, and they carry it with them throughout their medical careers. They believe they can find the tools to beat a disease, they can make a patient better. This is what drives them each day, it is who they are, and, quite frankly, it is who we want them to be.

The truth is, an unwavering, obsessive drive to extend life and defeat death is not such a bad trait in a doctor. In fact, that's just the kind of doctor we look for when we're diagnosed with a serious illness. We want a doctor who has enormous technical skill and is fanatic about fighting disease, one who will stay at work until all hours and lie awake nights figuring out how to solve the puzzle. We want a doctor who will save us.

The problem arises when we expect this same doctor, the one we sought out because he or she was so intent on finding a cure, to forget about blood cell counts and drug regimens, and talk instead about meaning at the end of life. It happens on television—a doctor blasts into the emergency room and saves the day, then spends long hours befriending and consoling patients and families. A doctor fights aggressively and then tempers that quest at exactly the right moment to become comforter, confidante, and sensitive counselor. On television, doctors understand human emotions as well as they understand antimetabolites and neutrophils. Some real-life doctors are like this. But most are not. It's a tall order, after all.

While we should push for better training of doctors, we also have to reexamine our own expectations, especially in light of the pressures that are brought to bear. At a time when lawmakers and corporations are trying to rein in escalating medical costs, we want doctors to spend more time listening to and counseling patients and their families. At a time when doctors have to be masters of physiology and pharmacology and advanced technology, we want them to serve as psychologist and pastor as well. At a time when one disease requires consultation with a number of specialists, and doctors often see patients for the first time when they are already in critical condition, we think they should develop a trusting and intimate relationship with patient and family.

Doctors should learn about palliative care. They should be able to talk about death with their patients. But we have to accept the limits of what they can be, and recognize the almost contradictory expectations we have of them. One minute we are pleading, "Do something," and the next minute we are asking, "Why didn't you stop sooner?" Medicine is filled with unknowns and uncertainties, and clouded further by fluctuating and profound emotions. Doctors need training in end-of-life care, but they cannot be all that we want them to be. And they cannot, by themselves, change the way we die.

This returns us to where we began: We have to accept some responsibility in creating kinder deaths for ourselves and our loved ones. Some of us may find the perfect doctor, but most of us will have to work with a doctor who will not speak openly and at length about death and who is not well-versed in palliative care. Most of us will have to work within the parameters of a medical system that is aimed at fighting illness and beating death.

What can we do? We can seek out a doctor who suits our needs, a doctor whom we trust and respect, and with whom we can speak openly. Then we can talk with that doctor about our views and preferences concerning end-of-life care, and make sure that he or she understands how important this issue is to us. We can have legal documents in place and be sure that our doctor not only knows about the documents but understands the intent behind them.

And then, when illness strikes, we need to initiate discussions and ask hard questions: *Where might this illness lead? What options will I have? What sorts of crises might arise? What will the end be like? How can we ease that process?* We have to give the doctor permission to be honest, and then push if he or she dodges our overtures. *This is extremely important to me. I need to talk with you about this.* When it comes to personal attention and care, we need to respect the demands on our doctors, but we also need to let them know what it is we want from them.

Finally, we have to appreciate our own role in shaping this passage. That role is not limited to asking questions and making sure a patient's treatment preferences are respected. We also have to open ourselves to the experience, the whole experience, taking part in it fully, so that the final act of life is not only merciful, but loving.

iv
brilliance in the
shadow of death

ars vivendi

the art of dying teaches us the art of living

And so we create a new *ars moriendi*, a death unhidden, a death reclaimed, a death in which loved ones are not looking on, helpless and awkward, but are actively involved. It is a death best kept out of the hospital, but which, in the end, has less to do with tubes and machines and more to do with openness, intimacy, forgiveness, and the rawest form of human love.

We know that we cannot design death in advance—a fact that is discomforting for a generation steeped in the desire for personal control—but we can help shape it. We can make it less frightening, painful, and lonely. We can surround it, share it, open ourselves to it.

Unfortunately, however, we cannot learn, or achieve, this art of dying in a day, we cannot address it in a single conversation, confirm it with a signature, or even acquire it by reading this book. It is a lesson we must study, and then revisit and rethink. We must keep it with us, in our being.

Perhaps we need woodcuts, like those from the 15th century, something we can look at, and study again and again. But in place of Satan's armies and clusters of angels battling it out, our modern-day prints will show bundles of tubes snaking their way seductively around respirators and heart monitors, appealing to our egos with promises of immortality, telling us that death can be fought and the battle won. On the other side, a simple bed at home surrounded by close friends and family, laughter and tears, quiet embraces, a reminder that we have another option, that there is another way.

Along with this imaginary woodcut, we must keep with us the knowledge of the choices we will face, for the lure of medical technology is a strong one. And more than anything else, we must keep with us the simple knowledge that no matter what we do or don't do, death will happen; we don't have the power to stop it, only the power to make it a little easier.

Unlike our ancestors, who knew death intimately and were reminded of it regularly, we are so insulated from death that we sometimes forget it even occurs and are stunned when confronted with it. But we need this knowledge, that death is real and unavoidable. Futile battles and the awkward silences often occur simply because something in us refuses to believe that death can happen, that we don't control it, we can't stop it. We have to accept, in whatever way we can, the reality and randomness of death, before we can change the way in which it occurs.

There is no need to obsess about death or to sit in constant dread of it. We simply need to be aware of it. Not just as some biological fact, but as a deeply felt truth, as a part of our lives and who we are.

We need to be aware that we will die and all the people who are important to us will die. Aware that, even as we color our hair and tone our bodies and try to smooth out our wrinkles, that this is a game, a pretense. We are mortal. All of us.

This awareness, present in the background of our lives, will enable us to think and speak more easily about death. It will help us to be a little more prepared, a little less surprised by it when we are confronted with it. And it will help us to change the way we die because it will change the way we live. It will affect all that we are, and all that we bring to that experience.

This is the bonus of this work, the magic we never expected; for studying the art of dying teaches us a second lesson, *ars vivendi*, the art of living. The reality of death—if we can see it, if we can resist the temptation to shut it out, close our eyes, and plug our ears—awakens us. It reminds us, loud and clear: *This is your life. Whatever you are going to make of it, do with it, get out of it, is happening right now.*

I have thought many times of Dennis Potter, the English writer who spoke of the "now-ness" of everything, the vividness and immediacy death had given his life. "In a perverse sort of way, I am almost serene," he said. I have thought of Dr. William Fair, former chairman of urology at Memorial Sloan-Kettering Cancer Center, who said, when his own cancer became terminal, that he was working to "expand" his life rather than trying to "extend" it. I have pictured my own father in the months before his death, staring in awe at a grain of sand or a blade of grass, and basking warmly in the laughter of his grandchildren. And I have wondered, Do we have to have a terminal diagnosis to achieve such insight? Do we have to be on the edge of life to value it? Aren't we all terminal? Aren't we all dying? Shouldn't we, can't we, expand our lives, appreciate the "now-ness" of everything, and celebrate this life, this very moment?

Of course we should. And we can, obviously not to the same degree as those who see death, who feel its chilly breath, but we can. In fact, when you study death and begin to accept it as a part of life, the expanding and now-ness happens almost without effort. Suddenly, you start living your life. Really living it. Enjoying it. Relishing it.

We will always get caught up in the irritations of the day. We will gripe at our spouses, worry about trivial things, snap at our kids, fall into bed feeling lonely and tired and sad. We will always despair and feel insecure and wrestle with anger. Life in all its ups and downs goes on. But when we are aware of death, we will have more of the other moments, moments when we realize how short it all is and how much, how very much, it all means. We will have moments when we stop and feel it, the life, the breath, the clarity. Moments when the big problems seem a little less big, and the mundane moments feel pretty damn good. We will walk away from the mess, or shrug at the sagging reflection in the mirror, or decide that a project can wait, and have another cup of coffee with a friend or just look at the world out the window and think that it is grand, quite grand, to be alive, for one more day.

It is a simple premise: we die well because we have lived well, and we live well because we know that we will die. This lesson has been preached, in one way or another, for hundreds of years by poets and philosophers. But because we are caught up in the day-to-day and so distanced from death, the lesson slips easily from our grasp.

Judy Hren is a hospice nurse who graciously allowed me to accompany her on her rounds for some time. I sat in the passenger seat as she navigated back roads in her blue, economy-size car. Most days she wore a pair of corduroys and a cotton shirt, with her thick brown hair pulled back in a long braid. Her lunch sat in a bag on the floor and was always eaten on the go. There is no time for a break; her day is full.

I watched as she met with one dying person, one grieving family after another, so easy and comfortable, as if she were simply stopping by to see old friends. Judy knows her patients' symptoms and medical histories and prognoses, but she also knows their whims and loves and annoyances. She knows who they used to be and who they are today. She knows their friends and where their children live and the name of the small brown collie who sits quietly by the door. She knows that she has to accept a cup of lukewarm, black coffee from this one's wife, and that another one will be tickled pink if she admires the family photographs that decorate the walls. I watched her hour after hour, talking so naturally with people who are dying, caring so gently for those who will soon be left behind.

One day I turned to her and asked, Isn't this work sad for you? "Sometimes," she said, "when someone touches you deeply and then they die." Is it depressing? "No. Not at all." She smiled. "You know, when my sons wrestle and put a hole in the Sheetrock or when my six-year-old sprays milk across the kitchen, it doesn't faze me. I know what's important. I come home and see five healthy kids, a husband, and I don't say anything, but I think, 'Geesh, look at all I have.'"

Death is horribly sad, but it is not simply a dark hole, an ugly pit into which we fall. Death is also a light, a brilliant light that shines on all the life that comes before, and all those days, those precious days, we have.

Most of us have a tendency to focus on the future, when we'll have more time or more money, a bigger house or a thinner body, when this task will be completed or that project will begin. We dream about having babies or an empty nest. We look forward to the retirement we imagine, or the success we crave, or the trip we read about in a magazine. But that tomorrow never comes, because we are always looking for something more and going someplace else; we are never exactly where we want to be.

Death reminds us that it is the journey itself, not some endpoint, that comprises life. For better or worse, every day we are doing it— not preparing for it, not gearing up for it, not practicing for it, but doing it. We pin our hopes on tomorrow, but death reminds us that we shouldn't put important things off. We can't postpone our dreams, our adventures, our apologies, our love, our friendships.

Remember Carol Tatkon, the executive who died of cancer? At one point in her illness, when an operation revealed that cancer had spread throughout her body, a doctor told Carol's family that she had about six months to live. "If there is anything she wants to do or anyplace she wants to go," he told them, "this would be a good time for her to do it." When Carol's sister passed on the doctor's advice to her, Carol responded without hesitation: "But I've been everywhere I want to go and I've done everything I want to do."

"That's the way she lived her life," her sister explained to me later. "She was up to date. She could have died at any time and there wouldn't have been these big things hanging over her. People talk about closure, but that's the way she lived her life. She didn't put things off and she didn't have any fences to mend."

How many of us can say the same?

Life and death curl around one another, inseparable, like the Chinese principles of yin and yang which together create a balance. Accepting our mortality is sad—even downright terrifying, at times —and yet taking hold of it, facing our fears, recognizing the inevitable and then learning about it, can also be liberating. It can make us realize that we don't have to be so afraid. We can prepare to some extent and ensure that our deaths will not be the nightmares we fear. And once we have done that, we can also live more fully, love more intensely, and forgive more readily, for we will live in the knowledge that all we have, all we have for sure, is today. We can find ourselves in this new place, still aware of where we're going, but also a little more appreciative of exactly where we are.

margaret

a lesson on living

It was April, but winter refused to loosen its grip. The night air felt cold, and old, like a guest who is no longer welcome. We scurried across the dark parking lot—my mother, my husband, my two-year-old son, Jack, and me—hugging our coats around us and stepping around the small puddles that pocked the black pavement. We entered the country club's front hall, shed our damp things, and headed for the dining room, pushing back our hair and adjusting our clothing as we went.

As soon as we got to the entrance, I saw Margaret standing behind the bar mixing drinks, and I headed straight for her. I love seeing Margaret. She radiates warmth and the most lovely sort of grace. Margaret is tall, has very blond, poofy hair, and wears thick black mascara. But the beautiful young girl she once was, 20 or 30 years ago, is still there, still apparent, beneath the years and the makeup. Margaret is the kind of person who lights up when she sees you, as if she has been missing you and is ever so glad to see you now, even though the truth is that she hardly knows you. And then, whoever you are, she listens intently to what you have to say as if it were the most interesting thing she has heard in some time. She laughs sweetly at your jokes and winks knowingly at your wisecracks and smiles at almost everything else, seeing whatever is good in you and, in doing so, helping you to see it too.

I love seeing Margaret because of all this, but mostly I love seeing Margaret because she did all of this for my father. She made him feel special. She made him feel young. She helped him sense the wonderfulness in himself. My father could be blunt and impatient and he could talk incessantly at times. Most people respected him as a doctor, and put up with him otherwise. But some people, like Margaret, saw beyond his prickly exterior to his soft innards. She saw a kind and sensitive man and she embraced him in his entirety. In doing so, in embracing this man, she embraced me too.

My parents used to go to this club on Friday evenings for the weekly cocktail hour and, in my single days when I lived nearby, I would sometimes meet them there. The drinks weren't free, but the stuffed mushrooms and mini-meatballs and barbecued ribs were, and Dad would eat enough to call it dinner. Being quasi-retired and not completely sure of what to do with his workday, he was usually the first to arrive. He would settle himself on one of the five barstools and Margaret would plant a bowl of mixed nuts in front of him and then make a whiskey sour in a tall glass, shake it up with ice, and decorate it with a slice of orange and a maraschino cherry. When bar business was slow, as it often was early in the evening, the two of them would talk and laugh, and she would call him Doctor with enormous respect and look at him with the most tender eyes, and Dad would melt at having such attention, especially from a tall, attractive woman with very blond hair.

As I walked into the room on that drizzly night, Margaret was plunking lipstick-red cherries into three fruity drinks and chatting with my mom, who had walked in a minute before me. Margaret looked up and gave me her I'm-so-happy-to-see-you smile, and I started to return it when I noticed my mother's stunned expression. Then I saw Margaret. Really saw her. It was a whittled-down Margaret. Emaciated. Anorexic. Her face was still pretty, but it was also gaunt. The thick blond hair that usually fell in waves around her face was now sparse and limp, pulled back with a hair elastic. The black bow tie of her uniform hung askew at her neck because there was nothing to hold it up. Her white shirt fell loosely on the bones of her narrowed shoulders, and tiny, angular wrists poked out of two open cuffs.

I knew what had happened before Margaret told me, but her explanation jolted me anyway because it was so blunt. "I have terminal cancer." She said it without embarrassment. She said it without anger. She said it without self-pity. She said it simply and factually, with just a hint of shared sorrow, as in "Oh well, some bad news. But there it is. What are you going to do?"

Margaret explained that she had gone for her annual physical eight months earlier, in August, and the doctor had given her a clean bill of health. But as she was leaving she mentioned that her ulcer was acting up again. A routine ultrasound revealed a pancreatic tumor the size of a golf ball and follow-up tests showed that the cancer had spread to other parts of her body. At that stage, pancreatic cancer typically kills its victims within six months, which would have given Margaret until February—two months earlier. At 53, Margaret, dear, sweet Margaret, was living on borrowed time.

As my mother went to find our table, Margaret told me about her illness and about her impending death. I hadn't mentioned my research; she simply had no qualms about talking about this subject. She was at ease, which put me at ease. I asked her what she was going through and she told me about her pain—minor, she said—about her chemo—she'd had some nausea, but not too bad—about her hair loss—thank God she still had most of it—and about her weight loss—"All my life I wanted to be thin and now I can't put on weight," she said with a chuckle. As she spoke, I stood in awe of her acceptance, her courage, and—as always with Margaret—her grace.

"I never felt, 'Why me?'" she said. "I never felt angry or that this was unfair. Life has ups and downs and this is my down. This is my time." She spoke softly and gently, as if not wanting to hurt me or jar me in any way. This illness, this dying, was something that she had accepted. These were the cards she had been dealt. She was not resentful or afraid.

I learned later that long before she became ill, Margaret had spoken openly about death many times. She said the usual things about not wanting to be kept alive on life support or with other aggressive medical treatments, but she went further than that, talking about cremation, her funeral, how she wanted to be remembered, and her thoughts on an afterlife. "She was very open about what she wanted," her daughter told me. "People would say, 'Are you planning on dying sometime soon?' And she would say, 'No. But it shouldn't be something that's scary to talk about. It's just a part of life. It's just the next stage.'"

Death, she believed, delivered you to some sort of life beyond and a reunion with others. And Margaret had plenty of others she was looking forward to seeing. She had lost three of her six siblings and at least one dear friend. One sister, who was also her very best friend, had died only a month earlier, in March, of a heart attack. While obviously upset over her sister's death, Margaret was also strangely soothed by it. It made her own death that much more bearable. As she explained it to me: "She's up there now, making a path for me."

No, Margaret wasn't afraid of death and she wasn't afraid of dying. Not really. She had cried a few times when she looked in the mirror and saw a face that she no longer recognized as her own. And she had been concerned about pain, but her doctor had assured her that he could keep her comfortable. She knew clearly where she was headed. Her concern was not for herself but for her 21-year-old daughter, Kim. Kim, she told me, was not taking this well.

In the time that I knew her, Margaret never spoke much about herself, but she spoke often about Kim, and when she did, she glowed. Kim was her baby, her pride, her reason for being.

Margaret herself had grown up in a basement apartment in the Bronx. Her parents were immigrants. Her father worked on the New York subways and her mother cleaned houses. Her family was poor and Margaret was deeply embarrassed by their poverty. So she worked hard to escape it, first by taking secretarial jobs, then through a modeling career, and eventually, after moving to Connecticut with her husband, at the country club. Her reward was a small house on the water, surrounded by roses, and a different kind of life for her only child.

Kim, who inherited her mother's beauty and femininity, was about to graduate from Boston College and was planning to go on from there to law school. It was Kim's graduation, this huge mark of success, that was keeping Margaret alive. She told her best friend that she was ready to die, but couldn't. She had to hang on to see her daughter get her diploma. In order to do that, Margaret did the unimaginable: She opted for surgery and underwent chemotherapy and its side effects. "Nothing was going to stop her," Kim said. "My mom was not a physically strong person, but I didn't realize how strong she was mentally. She told her doctor she was going to make it to my graduation. She said she couldn't die without leaving me settled."

Margaret and I were still talking when my little son, Jack, clamored up onto the barstool next to me. Margaret turned her attention to him, asking him about an oversized tie he was wearing (his grandfather's) while she mixed up a Shirley Temple with four cherries and two straws. She catered to him and elated him and captured him, just as she used to do with my father, his namesake. As I watched the two of them together, I couldn't help it, the tears began to stream down my face. My father was gone. Margaret was dying. She saw my face and turned to hug me. And then she looked into my eyes and said softly, "Maybe I'll see your dad soon."

I headed for the ladies' room.

The following month, Margaret achieved her goal. She made it to Boston for her daughter's graduation. Then it was just a matter of time. She had gotten her finances in order and redrafted her will. She was ready. She spent her final days tending to her beloved garden and enjoying the view of the sea from her porch. Slowly, she began to enclose her world, refusing to see most visitors and doing less each day.

One day in mid-July, Kim, who was spending the summer with friends in Rhode Island, noticed a change in her mother's voice as they spoke on the telephone. She drove home as soon as she could and arrived to find her mother in bed. Weak. Small. Quiet. Sickly. Life was draining out of her fast.

"You actually watch the person die right in front of you," Kim recalls. "You want to stop it but you can't. I thought, when I die the best way would be to have someone hold me and just be there, and not judge and not cry, because you're scared yourself. You don't need someone else pulling energy from you. My mother and I were alone in the room together, I was lying on the bed, holding her, and we were sharing stories. I was there for 48 hours straight, brushing her hair or making sure her Blistex was on, and keeping people away. I was adamant about no one coming into the room. It was a very private moment. My dad was in and out, but I wanted to be there every second. We'd been through so much together.

"My mother wasn't like a mom. We were so close it was amazing. Without a doubt, she was my best friend."

At such a young age, Kim was watching her mother/soulmate/ inspiration die, and was helping her to go. She watched death creep in, as her mother's body became thinner, as her legs and arms became cool, and her breathing became heavier. She watched her mother depart.

At one point Margaret awoke, slightly anxious. Her breathing was rapid. She pointed toward the corner of the room and said, "Look, look! It's so beautiful."

"I was like, 'Mom, I can't see anything,'" Kim said. "She was trying to share something with me and I couldn't see anything. Some people think that you hallucinate on morphine, but she was so convinced and she was so fully conscious that I can't believe it was a hallucination." After that vision, Kim said, her mother was much calmer and slept for longer intervals. She realized then that her mother was ready to go.

Late in the afternoon a day or two later Kim was lying with her mother while a few family members milled around. They started to talk about Margaret's death and Kim balked. "Hearing is one of the last things to go, so don't talk like that when you're in this room," she said. "Kim," they said to her, "maybe you have to let go." There was a frozen moment of silence and then Margaret, who had not moved in 24 hours, pulled her frail body on its side and lay one thin arm around her daughter's shoulders.

"It was amazing, how she got those long arms wrapped around me. I don't know how she did it," Kim said. "But that was my good-bye."

That night, when everyone was asleep and the house was quiet, Margaret took one last breath, paused, and then exhaled the last bit of air in her body. With that, she was gone.

"She looked absolutely beautiful," Kim says, sitting on her mother's porch, looking out over the gardens and seascape that her mother so loved. "She was in her own bed. She had this peaceful expression. She was beautiful."

Heeding Margaret's detailed instructions, her family cremated her and on the following Saturday, they held a party. Margaret did not believe in funerals, and especially disliked the idea of wakes. She wanted a party. She wanted people to celebrate. She wanted people to remember her as she was, alive and exuberant, not as someone dead and made-up to look alive. At the party, she insisted, there were to be no "funeral sprigs." People could bring a single yellow rose or make a donation to hospice.

Although Kim and her father expected a crowd, they never anticipated the hordes of people who came to celebrate Margaret's life and bid her farewell. Nearly 300 people jammed into her tiny house, most of them carrying a single yellow rose and a photo of Margaret.

"We had pictures of Mom and yellow roses all over the house," Kim recalled later. "It was definitely something she would have enjoyed. People were hanging out windows. There were limbs everywhere. There was laughter. People were sharing stories. It was an extreme tribute to her. The cards still haven't stopped. We have boxes upon boxes and we're trying to respond to them all but it's impossible. She touched a lot more people than I ever knew."

Obviously, Margaret's death changed Kim's life, but not simply because she lost her mother. The death itself, being part of that passage, was a turning point. "The whole experience gave me strength," she says. "There are some things you can't fight and the more you fight, the more miserable you'll be. I think that being close to someone and being there through the whole process helped me so much. It sounds eerie, watching someone die, but it was the best therapy for me. Facing it, what it brings. I know a lot of people saw my mom, a skeleton, saw her discomfort and then left the room and didn't know anything else. The only picture in their heads is, 'Oh my God, I'm going to deteriorate and be in such discomfort.' But when you're there through the whole process, you see that that is just a minor part of it. The rest of it is coming to terms and having your good-byes.

"The best therapy for us was the laughter. She and I loved to laugh together. Even toward the end, we were laughing. Those are the memories that we share."

My own final memory of Margaret was that night at the country club. We spoke by phone after that, but I never saw her again.

After dinner, I went to say good-bye to Margaret while my mother took Jack exploring. The two of them found a doorway behind the bar which led to a large hallway with a grand chandelier. They decided that they were in a ballroom and began to dance. Jack's striped oxford shirt hung out on one side, one of his red Keds had come untied, and his green baseball cap was turned sideways on his blond head. Holding hands with his grandmother, he swirled and laughed and pranced wildly about the room.

Margaret and I stood together, watching them. "My mother taught me that you have to become innocent again," she said, not taking her eyes from the dancing pair. I looked at her for a moment, confused. "You have to bring yourself back to your childhood," she explained, "to get that innocence, to accept people fully, the way children do."

"Do you have to see death, be close to death, before you can do that?" I asked.

"No," she said. "You work your whole life trying to do that."

Margaret did it. She achieved that innocence, and in doing so was one of the most accomplished people I have ever met. She accepted people, found the good in them, and relished life. She was pure and unfettered.

Someone once told me that some people are like shooting stars. We look out and see them for a moment against the dark sky and we say "aahhh." And then they are gone. A life so brief, and yet so brilliant. Margaret was, for me, a flash of starlight, a wonder and an inspiration. I don't know if she is reunited with her siblings and friends, handing out maraschino cherries at a party of the everlasting—I certainly hope she is—but I know for a fact that she lives on, lives on and on, in all that she was and all that she gave to others. A life well lived; a death full of love. What more can we ask for?

index